I'VE TOLD YOU THIS ONE, HAVEN'T I?

James B Doohan

TITLE: I'VE TOLD YOU THIS ONE, HAVEN'T I?

ISBN: 978-0-6454042-1-0 Paperback
ISBN: 978-0-6454042-6-5 eBook

ILLUSTRATIONS: Gary Bell

FIRST PUBLISHED: 2022

Published with the assistance of Angel Key Publications
https://angelkey.com.au

Angel Key Publications

The cover shot is of an iceberg taken by James Doohan on the way to the Antarctic in January 1966. It was taken from the deck of The Nella Dan. This iceberg is the size of two city blocks and the Ship's rules are that they must stay at least 1.6km (One mile) away from these big bergs. This one is about 2kms away from the photographer and even at that distance the sea is seething around the ship. What is shown is only 1/5th of the berg as 4/5ths are under the water.

Contents

With love to my wife June of 55 years -
beautiful, talented and enduring of my
eccentricities, for so long.

Foreword

When I handed the draft of my book *'The Sniveller's Handbook'* to my editor/publisher in 2000, he remarked, 'Everybody's got a story, Jim.' At eighty, the conversational age, I now know what he meant. Of course, I have many exciting stories to tell, but so does everybody else. There is no reason to think that my stories are any more than monotonous dirges - that struggle to raise people's heads above the parapet of their ubiquitous smartphones.

I have written a few stories about memorable incidents, from my struggles to master an ex-racehorse at nine year's old to some funny incidents emanating from my Army life, and one just had to be told about an audacious fellow officer.

There are just six stories in that ilk (enough then); throughout my past life, there is more that I could ramble on about, but really, who cares? Four of the six stories have been previously published in various papers and magazines, showing credibility. Perhaps on reflection, the editors needed some padding. I have now grouped them into one book as my feeble contribution to the literal world

I have been prevailed upon by acquaintances to republish my book, 'The Sniveller's Handbook,' now out of print for fifteen years, all original copies sold.

I have decided to use a reprint of *'The Sniveller's Handbook'* on the reverse end of the short stories for the economy and sheer laziness. Pretty clumsy, really, but as my wily Greek mate says, 'it is what it is.'

I hope you enjoy it.

James B

My friend of thirty plus years, Gary Bell, the cartoonist, recently confessed to me that he always wanted to be a cartoonist. However, national service for his country and the outstanding Army Officer that he turned out to be interrupted his true craft.

Now a successful artist and world traveller, he has been enticed to add some quality into my stories with cartoons. His cartoons also appear throughout my Sniveller's Handbook, and I am afraid Gary's inflicted with the same sick irreverent view on life that I have. Gary's cartoons leave the words that follow in the story redundant. God bless him.

Gary

I CALLED HIM BAMBI THEY CALLED HIM RADISH

I suppose I was no more than four years old on the day we all stood around looking at the foal gamely, trying to stagger to his feet. We were all there, Dad, Mum, my two big brothers, my sister and me. He had long gangly legs which crumpled under him every time he tried to stand, while his dam, 'the brown mare' nuzzled him encouragingly.

He looked great with his light fawn colour, a blaze on his forehead and four white socks. 'That's my little Bambi,' I squeaked. Although the rest of the family smiled tolerantly, 'spoiled brat' was getting in for his chop again. 'Bambi' came from my tattered, much-loved book I went to sleep with every night.

So, Bambi, he was.

That was until he became officially registered for racing and formally christened 'Merigan Prince', sire 'Calshot' and dam 'Brown Mare' as my father inelegantly called her.

That's how he became a racehorse, well, a sort of a race-horse. He did win his maiden and an incredible string of seconds. 'Would have been a bloody champion if he wasn't injured when they were breakin' him in,' I heard my dad mutter morosely from time to time.

Getting second places on country tracks don't pay for the chaff, so he came home at four years old.

Once off the chaff and the excellent fare, his condition deteriorated. I described it confidentially to my friends as 'fine'. 'Bambi just doesn't carry any weight at all.' My friends said he was skinny.

Around that time, a popular Sunday Newspaper started featuring a comic strip about a thin decrepit racehorse called Radish. It had to happen, and it did; my very insensitive uncle Felix dubbed him Radish. It stuck. Oh, sure, I was brave about it, firmly calling him Bambi (I never did like that highfalutin 'Merigan Prince'). I had a kind sister who called him Bambi too. Everyone else called him Radish.

For a few **months** after **Bambi returned home to us, we all carefully** walked around him *a* bit. He looked huge compared to Sox, the **chestnut stock horse I rode to school** every day. Not that Sox was terrible; in fact, **he** had a fair turn of speed on the way home from school, compared to the other kid's horses. Still, he took a while **to** warm up, and I had lost a lot of races - because of that.

Admittedly the races were only spontaneous ones, for example, to Bruce Knapp's cream box, from where some enterprising contestant starter should happen to be able to catch the rest of us unawares. (Just as when he finished, and we were still sitting side-saddle munching on handfuls of mulberries that we swiped from Adam's tree). However, it inevitably gave him a valuable break before we realised what was happening, until whooping like a **band of** Indian's we would head **off** after him, only to lose the race by a couple of lengths.

Still, this **was** a sports model. By gosh, I'd show 'em, Radish? They'd have to call him Bambi after the lickin' I'd give 'em on him. But, of course, Dad would have none of it. 'You're jokin', ride him to school, why you'd kill yourself!' So, I rode Sox, the other kids jeered, and I smarted over it.

Bill, my big brother of fifteen, finally plucked up courage and rode him one day. Struth, you orta have seen him take off! He was just fine when walking along slowly, but Bill suddenly got game and booted him in the ribs. The clods flew as his back legs skitted a few times, getting a grip in the soft mud, and then off they went, like a GTHO Ford taking off at the lights. Bill started by hanging onto the reins with one hand, trying like steam to pull him up. His other hand firmly clamped onto his battered old grey felt hat as the wind rushed past him, but he hadn't gone a hundred yards when he panicked, let go of the hat and grabbed the reins with both hands. Next, he was standing up in the stirrups shouting, 'whoa, whoa, you fergin, blankety, blank', as he disappeared around the corner of the hill, a half-mile **away.** Dad shook his head and snorted in disgust, 'no bloody cows away. I told him to round them up, not go out the back paddock looking for some'.

A half-hour later, Bill returned, leading Bambi. **So,** nobody rode him again for a long while.

Being hungry dairy farmers, we ate a lot of bread. The bus delivered the bread to the neighbour's cream box about a mile away, down a narrow-rutted lane. It was my job to get it every couple of days before breakfast by riding **Sox down** and back.

Then came **the** day that I couldn't catch Sox. He was a wily old devil and had managed to get out of the horse paddock.

The brown mare, which I was allowed to ride 'on occasions', was also gone. So that left Bambi, back legs crossed, eyes closed and drowsing contentedly under the big old wild apple tree at the bottom of the yard.

'You'll have to walk, Harry,' Dad said, matter of factly.

I wasn't having any of that, as far as I could see, here was a perfectly good horse, just itching to be ridden, and besides, Mum was waiting for the bread now, I pointed out with a devastating show of logic.

Dad shrugged non-committedly, which I realised with a cold grip of fear up my backbone was probably some form of consent.

So, I shook out the bridle and approached Bambi, still dozing under the apple tree. He didn't wake when I grabbed his mane, so I slipped the bit between his teeth and Presto, the bridle was on! He woke when I yanked on the bridle to lead him over to a large stump where I could climb onto his sixteen and a half hands. Though, I noticed the wicked look in his eye at this stage. Sort of a slumbering volcano, all capped and ready to go. Right then, I thought it just might be best to walk after all. 'Sock it to 'em, Jimmy', my kind-hearted sister yelled as she and my two elder brothers walked out from the bails to watch the performance. Fortunately for me, they were too far away to see my white putty-like face and trembling hands as I slithered on top of him, bareback, of course. The trip to the cream box was dead slow. My dog Smokey usually raced me, he could beat Sox easily, but he was disgusted today as we plodded along. After whining discontentedly at our heels for about half a mile, he headed off up a gully we had crossed to try and stir up some rabbits.

I knew I was in a real fix when I reached the cream box. There was no way I could stand the shame of having walked Bambi down and back home again. It would have just about been faster walking.

I pondered this as I stuffed the bread, and, oh, I nearly forgot, there was an oversized parcel of meat that day, too, into the sugar bag. There were three big double loaves of bread and a parcel of meat. There was just a dog's ear corner of the sugar bag left for me to hold on to it. While loading the bag, I kept looking at Bambi, dozing passively with the reins on the ground. *Surely, he can't be that bad*, I thought to myself.

When we started heading back, he pricked his ears for a while, but he soon realised that I was firmly committed to a walk, so he wigwagged his ears a bit and kept up a steady plodding gait walking the two hundred and fifty yards or so until we reached the causeway at the corner of the hill. At this point, I writhed in embarrassment, for as we dawdled around the hill, we swept in full view of the yard. My ears burned as I thought I could hear Bill's raucous remarks from even eleven hundred yards away.

We plodded on for another fifty yards; until I knew that nothing could be worse than to walk home all the way. *I'll just trot 'im a bit*, I thought. So, experimentally I gently dug a bare heel into Bambi's ribs. Both of his eyes opened wide, and his ears shot forward, the 'clunk to clunk' sound of his hooves sharpened to a kind of 'clickity, clickity, clickity'. It was faster, I knew, with my heart skipping several beats, but what I needed was a trot. It was right then that I made my worst mistake. I booted him fair and square in the ribs with both feet. His lunge was about nine and a half yards from where he stood before. The reins slithered through my hands like the anchor chain dropping on the USS Missouri, and I was suddenly sitting on his rump, scrabbling wildly to stay on.

His second lunge was even greater, and I foolishly gathered him in. I bet in his mind's eye right then; he could see the white rails of the racetrack flashing by, as he started in earnest about then. Somehow, I managed to hang onto the sugar bag for the next half-mile grimly. I know it was the sheer terror that kept my death's grip on the corner of the bag. I realised I was still holding it only when the mouth of the bag opened, and a stream of sausages, pork chops and rump steaks whizzed over my shoulder. It was promptly followed by one, two and three loaves of bread until I was left clutching an empty bag flapping madly in the wind. I was too frightened to fall off. All I could do was sit tight and pray that he could take the ninety-degree bend from the laneway into our gateway at the blinding pace he was going.

Boy, was he good! Without missing a beat, he did a sort of one-legged side slip through the open gate and thundered furiously up to the yard where he screeched to a sliding stop, sending me spearing over his head, over the top rail of the yard and headfirst into the mud. When I sat up covered in mud, everyone was crying. Well, they were rolling around on the grass with tears streaming down their faces anyway. Even Dad was howling with laughter. Even now, every time I think of it, my face turns red, and I leave the room when old-time reminiscences bring it up.

Meanwhile, Bambi was seen contentedly cropping grass, with what I am sure was a satisfied sneer on his mouth. I didn't ride him for a long while after that.

Youth gives one certain persistence. So, the problem of riding Bambi, or more importantly, controlling him, became my obsession, and I was determined to show all those detractors that I could do it.

My brother Bill, older and much stronger, and a bit of a daredevil, helped the process quite a bit by riding him, albeit cautiously, around the farm. We all stood and gave raucous jeering cheers whenever he lost control. Then, Bambi bolted and came to a screeching halt in front of us up at the yard, sending great clods of mud flying ahead of him. Bill, white-faced, while he flashed us a sickly grin, tried to appear calm about it all. However, this sort of 'control' did little to lessen our apprehension about riding Bambi.

As a young male chauvinist, my sister Mary irritated me. I think Bambi fancied her; she brown-nosed to him, calling him 'Bambi', his favourite name incidentally. He was smart enough to know that 'Radish' was a derogatory name, and he disliked it intensely. Bill, of course, always referred to him as Radish. I'm sure that's why they never really did get on.

It was Mary who made the initial breakthrough, though she insisted on using a large, heavy stock saddle, an implement I disdained as unable to get the 'feel' of the horse when you used it. At least that was my claim. Everybody else claimed I was too weak to throw it on him. Mary, I must admit, for a girl or anyone else for that matter, was just about fearless. She was a great asset on a cricket team and was usually the first pick when choosing sides. Generally, she toughed it out well with her three brothers, who didn't take to wimps kindly.

She started on him riding over the creek to our grand-mothers about a mile away. Cunning move that, as Bambi was forced to stop at gates, as he was just about to 'get into stride'. There were two gates, and the road or track between gate one and gate two was where she 'opened him up a bit'. Nothing sensational, just a quick burst of a furlong or so, which must have been frustrating for him.

Next, over our mother's vigorous protestations, she proposed a visit four miles away to one of our many cousins, who was a close friend. Her means of locomotion. Bambi, of course. Mary confessed to me later that it was a slow trip; she only opened him up from the road to her cousin's place, which was perched high up on a hill. This distance was about three hundred yards.

Mary became reasonably competent at riding him after that. I remember watching her when she rode past the school, often at play lunch. First, we would hear Bambi clattering up the road, and then he would sweep into view just before a bend in the road opposite the church, two hundred yards further along from the school.

He inevitably attacked the bend like a formula one racing car, cutting into the curve by just missing the white post on the ditch at the curve's centre and then running out wide on the way out of the bend, using every bit of the road to perfection. Mary leaned in the saddle with her brown hair streaming out behind her. I don't know whether she was aware of us as an audience, but I used to watch her and Bambi, my heart full of pride. Yes, now they could see what Bambi could do; no sling offs at me about the 'skinny' horse anymore.

The other kids watched surreptitiously. Oh, they knew horse and rider were spectacular, all right. There wasn't one of them who hadn't grown up on a horse, usually starting to ride by the time they were three years old, and there wasn't one of them who didn't wish they were right up there like Mary, pounding down the road. So, I contented myself with a superior satisfied smile at these times; I loved this sweet revenge for all those jeers. The only trouble was it wasn't me riding him. I still got teased about that.

Unfortunately, Mary was attending boarding school and only came home at the term's end. It was drastic as Bambi was ridden only during school holidays. So, the only way I would learn to control him was in the school holidays, after Mary had 'softened him up' a bit.

After pondering the problem for some time, I finally remembered how Mary had begun—riding over to grandmas? But, no, that was too risky for me. I shuddered as I thought what would happen if he did a quick whirl and scoot as I was leaning over off him, trying to shut one of the gates. The answer was the hill; if I picked one carefully, that could make the difference.

One afternoon, soon after I had arrived at this conclusion, Dad told me to fetch some stray cows, and Sox was missing. Instead, there stood Bambi, dozing under the apple tree. Cautiously I shook out the bridle and approached him. No reaction, just a sort of 'ho hum, here we go again' look. Except

I thought I detected a predatory glint in his eye when he realised it was I, not Mary, who was fiddling with the harness.

Tugging on the reins, I dragged him over to the stump where I could get the necessary height to struggle onto his back. Dad opened the rails for me to get through and said, 'See ya, son,' in a mournful voice that made me swallow nervously.

I headed 'out the back' ('the back' being around the corner of the main ridgeline of hills that ran through our farm) where the missing cows were.

We walked the quarter mile or so to the corner of the hill, out of view of the yard. Taunts of 'good on you, speedy' and 'look at flash go' burned in my ears all the way.

I reined him up on rounding the corner and surveyed the route carefully. Yonder to my right was a small hillock *that will do nicely to steady 'im*, I thought as I gigged him in the ribs and pointed him towards it.

Bambi's ears shot forward in joy '*oh boy*,' I could almost hear him say to himself, *'this is your life mate, let's gooooo'* and straightaway, he lunged into a gallop.

The wind whistled past my ears; my old serge coat was wildly flapping as I clung on desperately. We headed straight for the hillock, which Bambi rumbled up and over without missing a beat. As we went over the hillock, I panicked. It had failed to slow him, and the only way to stop him was to head for the fence junction near a gully about a half-mile away, so I guided him there.

Gleefully he raced through the blady grass, leaping over logs in his path and scattering the half dozen stray cows clustered along the trail in his wake. I kept yelling, 'whoa, whoa you rotten stinkin,' while I sawed futilely on the bit, but that only made him go faster.

We swept across a small green flat just before the fence corner that I could guide him towards with what bit of control

I had. He saw the fence at the last minute and tried to swerve, but he realised he couldn't make it at sixty yards out, and he put on the brakes. Boy, did he put on the brakes! He slammed down on his haunches and slid on his rump while I grabbed a great handful of his mane and held on like a leech. He stopped with inches to spare, with me dangling up around his neck, which was drooping over the fence. Behind me, the telltale skid marks went for fifty yards.

I dismounted then and sat down, my legs were like putty, and my heart was going at ninety miles an hour. So, we went home with the cows dead slow. The campaign had been a complete abysmal failure.

It was three weeks before I dared to plan again how to tackle him.

This plan centred around a ridge that ran towards the gully from the main ridgeline out the back. It ended in a dreadfully steep peak. *I wonder?* I thought as my eye caught sight of it one day while hunting for strays on Sox. and I surveyed it carefully.

Looking back to where Bambi had started his burst last time, I saw it was about two furlongs away from the peak, and boy, what a mountain! It was as steep as Cheops pyramid where he'd have to tackle it; even the trees grew on it at right angles, standing out like a giant ladder all the way up.

It was so steep the cattle shunned it; therefore, there was no problem with cattle tracks on it. My only worry was if Bambi lost forward momentum on the way up, he would fall over backwards, almost. But boy oh boy, what a beaut anchor!

Mary was due to go back to boarding school soon, so I approached her innocently and asked if she would see her cousin again before then. 'Tomorrow,' came the reply, and I could have leapt for joy. That trip would soften him up nicely.

The day after that was the day I would put into action plan B, plan A, having been my spectacular failure of three weeks before.

This is it, Jimmy, I thought as I approached Bambi, contemptuously bypassing Sox as I walked purposefully to where he stood in his favourite position under the apple tree. Dad gawked at me in disbelief as I walked past and took off his old felt hat while he scratched his head in perplexity.

Dad's comment of 'sure you know what you're doin', son?' rattled me somewhat, but I firmly pressed on without answering. The others in the yard were strangely silent as I walked towards the corner; they undoubtedly wondered what I was doing.

We started at a slow walk with Smokey scouring the gullies and ridges looking for the odd rabbit, Bambi, meanwhile, plodded along in a disinterested way; he had nothing but contempt for riders who merely walked him. He showed it in the way he casually swung his front hooves in a sort of exaggerated arc, which scuffed through the dust and sent clouds billowing up around his front legs. I'm sure this was his source of amusement, as everything else was boring to him.

When we rounded the corner, I reined him to a halt, gathering the reins carefully. Instantly his ears pricked forward, and his eyes brightened. Then aiming him for the peak, I had christened Cheops, I booted him in the ribs.

He took a tremendous lunge from a standstill, with his back legs skittering a couple of times to gain purchase. Although to me, it felt like the blasting thrust from the rocket motor on the X-15 rocket plane, I knew I was ready, but even so, I ended up sliding back onto his rump as he took off.

As I squirmed forward by dragging myself up with the reins, he continued accelerating, but fortunately for me, we headed straight towards Cheops. At the base of the peak, he was still warming up his run. I'm sure he hadn't really noticed the hill. Before I knew it, we were scrambling up the mountain with no loss of momentum. It was fantastic - he came up that almost vertical peak for nearly seventy-five yards without missing a beat. I started to worry again, but then joy as I felt a slight slowing in his stride until we arrived at the top of the ridge with all his pace gone.

On the summit, I pulled him up effortlessly, and he stood there blowing furiously, glancing around at the steep ascent as if to say, 'What the hell was that?'

Going off the ridge at an easy angle, I gigged him in the ribs, and he trotted meekly down to the flat. So, this was my day; I was elated!

I gigged him twice to test him further, and he broke into a canter - yep, that's right - a canter. I didn't even know he had such a gait before. It was a beautiful rocking canter, nearly as fast as Sox in full flight but nowhere near as uncontrolled as his gallop. When I pulled on the reins, he quickly came to a halt, glad of the rest; I'm sure because that hill climb really had been something.

This was control, almost absolute control. But I wasn't kidding myself – Bambi was only taking a breather. Meanwhile, I was going to revel in it. One thing, tractable he might be now, but I'd need that hill again every time I rode him.

That day I rounded up the cows and had them back in quick time. My exhibition was complete when one tried to break away just before we herded them into the yard, and I was able to canter Bambi after her and bring her back.

No one at the yard spoke a word. They knew something had happened. But they weren't going to ask what. So, until now, I have never told anyone what happened. For sixty-eight years, I have remained smug about it.

SABRINA

Sabrina was born in 1936 and died in 2016. Sabrina was the British answer to Marilyn Monroe and enjoyed stardom in the 1950s. Her arrival in Australia in the 1950s elucidated a welcome compared with the Beatles' reception years later. 'Sabrina Land' is named in her honour, in the Australian portion of the Antarctic, due to her visit to the departing 1959 ANARE Expedition. A DUKW was also named after her – explained in the story below.

The following resulted from a suggestion to write a story about my recollections of my time in the Antarctic. There were many to choose from, but I settled on this story. This story is by far the best; too good not to see the light of day. Some would say – this is one of the most entertaining yarns to come out of the corps' history in peacetime.

Before proceeding, I would remind the reader that these events took place some sixty years ago. I have done a good deal of research to preserve its integrity and infused the story with my experience (gained from two trips to the Antarctic in 1965/6/7). The story needed to be more than a boring narrative; I have relied on hearsay and conjecture to ensure its flow and readability.

I apologise to the reader for any conjecture that may have distorted facts that occurred.

THE SABRINA AFFAIR

Wednesday the 7th of January 1959: The DADST picked up the morning papers and, smiling, studied the pictures. A DUKW was on the wharf, Sabrina smashing a champagne bottle against the hull and the polar ship Magga Dan fully loaded, ready to sail, on the front page. More photos of huge crowds on the following pages: Sabrina and Lt Willing were looking at a map of Antarctica and various other poses.

He tucked the paper under his arm and walked softly along the corridor, quietly checking to see if the CRASC had returned from the GOC's morning conference. Then, satisfied that his office was empty, he nodded to the secretary and, upon entering the room, carefully placed the paper on the CRASC's desk, positioning it so he could not miss the story.

Wheeling around, he walked out, softly closing the door behind him, nodding again to the secretary who was busy at her typewriter. He headed back to his office, glancing at his watch as he did so, almost ten o'clock; it was time for morning tea at the Mess.

As he approached his office, the other officers were making their way up the corridor towards the Mess for the traditional morning tea at that time.

Once inside, he took time to watch for Col Dowdy, which didn't take long. There he was, gimlet blue eyes peering out under the brim of his cap, striding up the corridor towards his office, reciprocating the officers salute as he passed them, with a short, barely noticeable, nod. He grasped the handle of his office door and walked inside.

'Should be about now!'

'Aaaaaaarrrggghhhh!' A banshee howl of rage echoed stridently down the corridor.

'I'm out of here', and he scuttled past the commander's closed door. Just as he was starting up the Officer's Mess steps, he heard the Col's door wrench open and his voice yelling urgently, 'Gordon! Gordon!'

Close - but he had got away just in time.

The CRASC came striding into the Mess, ripped his red-banded cap from his head and jammed it on a cap hook so viciously that the shape distorted, and the hook almost protruded through the fabric. An audible titter ran through the Mess then quickly ceased. All talking stopped; it was quiet.

He stood there scowling, his thin white moustache bristling in anger, looking for someone, anyone on whom to vent his rage. Instead, all the RAASC officers attempted to make themselves inconspicuous by shrinking into the background. Everyone avoided eye contact with him, craving anonymity.

The GOC greeted him smilingly. 'Hi Vin, I see one of your young corps' officers made the front page?' Dowdy strangled a grunt in reply and snatched two toasted sandwiches from a silver tray, borne by a passing steward, immaculate in his white coat. He was taking quick little bites from the sandwich. He swivelled his head around, looking out under his lowered brow; sparks seemed to fly from his bushy white eyebrows.

A well-liked figure, admired and held in esteem, but with an explosive temper and being very strait-laced, the lurid newspaper articles struck at the core of his beliefs. The mess members knew it; they could have predicted his exact reaction. They would have been sorely disappointed if he had reacted otherwise. Nevertheless, they were fascinated by his exhibition.

Just then, a breathless steward came running up - 'Col Dowdy, the CGS is on the line for you in the mess sergeant's office, sir!'

Swallowing hard, he straightened his shoulders and stalked towards the office. An awed silence gripped the room.

Reluctantly, he picked up the phone, 'Hello, Dowdy speaking,' Ah, Vin. Ragnar here.

'Yes. Hello, sir.'

'I've just had a call from the Governor-General.'

Dowdy gagged and stiffened, his knuckles stark white as he tightened his grip on the telephone.

In late 1965, I arrived at the Australian National Antarctic Research Expedition (ANARE) headquarters. I was handed an impressively thick Antarctic Manual in colour during our weeklong pre-embarkation briefing. On thumbing through the pages, I saw a picture of a DUKW in the water at Wilkes, flanked by the ubiquitous 'bergy bits' (mini icebergs), and the caption read 'Lt Dick Willing in his DUKW at Wilkes Base'.

Photo: A. CAMPBELL-DRURY

Top: An Army Dukw transfers diesel fuel from the expedition's supply ship to Wilkes during the annual relief of ANARE stations.

The DUKW Sabrina at Wilkes Antarctica

What intrigued me was the name of the DUKW, *'SABRINA'* in pink writing emblazoned across the bow of the DUKW. I thought it strange because the strict policy was all expedition DUKWs were named after a serving or recently retired senior officer. Furthermore, the RAASC Corps Directorate allocated the names very deliberately. So, for the life of me, I could not imagine nor think of an officer named Sabrina.

Turning to Alan Campbell-Drury, who had put the manual together and was the ANARE official photographer at the time, I asked him to explain.

His roar of laughter encouraged Doug Twigg, the communications expert, to join him. He and Doug had similar long histories with the department and knew its history well. Looking at the photograph and laughing, they regaled me with the story.

Major Richard T Willing MBE was the most dynamic officer I had encountered in twenty-four years of service. He would have made Beau Brummell green with envy with his elegant dress sense. He was the only officer I ever knew who looked good in the old Australian Army Battle Dress.

Wherever Dick went, everything frothed and bubbled around him. He was a mixture of Beau Brummell, Peter Pan and Clark Kent with his horned rimmed glasses. In any situation, he was a constant source of perplexity to his senior officers and idolised by us junior officers with his sangfroid. On the other hand, he was irresistible to the opposite sex of all ages with his charm and grace. In summary, Major Dick Willing MBE was 'One Cool Cat'.

He graduated from RMC in Dec '57 and straightaway went to the RAASC School at Puckapunyal, where he spent the next few months on a young officer's course.

Upon completing the course in May '58, he was posted to 11 Training Battalion in Wacol Qld for a few months until he was attached to HQ DST in Melbourne for duties with ANARE. Their headquarters were in St Kilda Melbourne.

Dick had significant advantages over mere mortals who fearfully tread more sedate paths with his smooth style and audacious nature. You could say that he would 'charge hell with a bucket of water' and look good doing it.

His audacity was amply demonstrated on two occasions, the widely acclaimed 'Sabrina Affair'; and later in Brunei, where he wrested back control of an airfield single-handed, totally demoralising a rebel force in the process. Then, with a fierce demeanour etched on his face and in reckless abandon of his safety, he exploded out of an aircraft waving his nine millimetre Browning around, catching the rebels by surprise who fled in terror, abandoning the airfield. For this conspicuous, and others would say foolhardy action, he earned a 'good MBE'.

Others said he should have earned an MBE earlier for enticing Sabrina, the forty-one and a half, seventeen, thirty-six-inch curvaceous, famous British blonde actress and the toast of Melbourne at the time, to christen his DUKW after her, before he departed for Antarctica.

Sabrina had first come to the attention of young army officers when she appeared in a bit part in a British training film on 'Methods of Instruction'. The lesson brought out in her appearance was about 'not having distractions to the class'. Flash the scene to a major with his pointer tapping at the blackboard, while twenty-two students are sitting glumly at their desks when a beautiful blonde walks past the open window sporting an enormous bosom and voluptuous curves. Twenty-two heads snap around, and twenty-two pairs of eyes riveted on the figure of Sabrina as she vamps past, swivelling her hips in an ostentatious parade. Suddenly, in a rush to the window, desks tipped over, and the lesson ends in chaos – cut – 'how not to do it.'

Before the ANARE Army detachment could embark on the Danish polar ship, the Magga Dan, a mountain of work needed completion in readiness. The preparation of the vehicles for operations in such a ferocious climate, using special oil additives. Such as greasing the Higgins and Gould pump chains with sticky Molybond grease, undoing the sixty-eight nuts on the outer wheel rim, recoating them with Kopr Kote grease, and retightening them (there are six wheels on each DUKW). Then, assessing the DUKWs thoroughly before undertaking training operations with ANARE on Port Phillip Bay. Simultaneously ordering and sorting out the vast range of spares before packaging and marking them carefully and in addition, finishing all administrative details before sailing.

Once the ship sailed, communication to Australia was limited to the ships radio officer and teletype printouts - in code to limit traffic. Hence meticulous administrative preparations were essential as no corrections were possible after sailing. It was a punishing schedule, but fortunately, the nights were free, and while the money lasted, Melbourne was at the detachment's mercy. With Dick Willing on the loose, that meant 'Melbourne watch out'.

At the same time, Sabrina was performing in Melbourne at the Tivoli. By now, a superstar, her drawing power set a record on arrival in Melbourne, not broken until five years later by the Beatles in 1964.

A singular feature of Dick's character was his old-fashioned virtue of sticking rigidly to the motto 'a gentleman never talks about his lady acquaintances.' Others may gossip or gloat, never Dick. Therefore, no titillating facts or salacious details of how Dick met Sabrina and chatted her up are available. One can only speculate on his tactics.

Dick's good looks and perfect dress always stood out so that he would have easily caught her attention during her Tivoli act. If he alluded subtly to his forthcoming daring adventure to the great white wasteland, he would instantly become an object of interest, unique which would set him apart. It was a clever tactic.

Every Brit those days had heard the story of the daring but ill-fated, 'Scott of the Antarctic.' How his fateful last trip when every expedition member to the South Pole perished. It created an inbuilt apprehension of the dangers of Antarctica and built-up Dick's 'bravery' credentials in her eyes. In addition, the word 'expedition' as in 'The Australian National Antarctic Research

Expedition' had a certain ring to it which no doubt she found fascinating.

So, having gained her rapt attention, how to maintain it? 'I know I'll call my DUKW 'Sabrina' in honour of you, and you can christen it the day we leave.' Could any conscious publicity star resist such a carrot? Absolutely not! Her publicity crew seized on this opportunity to expand and enhance her image, ensuring all the news media outlets were on alert for the impending dramatic event, staged on the day the Magga Dan was to sail for Wilkes.

Dick now had to overcome the not so trivial matter of omitting the Army allocated name of V E Dowdy on his DUKW and inserting Sabrina's name instead. Even thinking about it was breathlessly audacious and would make the bravest heart quail. Col V E Dowdy just happened to be the CRASC Southern Command based in Victoria Barracks Melbourne within walking distance of Dick's Sturt Street depot where his detachment was based. Junior officers in the headquarters trembled at the sound of Col Dowdy's steps in the corridor, praying he was not visiting them for a dressing down. He had a tongue like a whiplash. I know as I experienced it in the earliest stage of my career when I objected to my initial posting.

A fair, stern man, his temper was legendary. When summoned on the intercom to his office, his staff officers demanded he put down his swagger stick before they dared appear before him. No one knew whether the 'Vin' was short for 'Vincent' or 'vinegar'. Strictly religious, with a solid moral code, he expected the highest ethical standards from all the corps officers, especially junior officers. But, to usurp his name with that of a well-endowed actress! The mind boggles.

No wonder Dick informed very few people of his plans, neglecting to seek permission – just proceeded to quietly have a sign writer emblazon the name *SABRINA* in beautiful sizeable pink writing across the bow of his DUKW. Then two more sombre renditions of Sabrina on each side of the DUKW level with the driver's seat. All carefully concealed under draped covers until dramatically revealed during the christening ceremony. Worry, why bother? Dick was never one to worry about consequences. He maintained stoically that it could only happen once to you unless you worried, then it could happen a thousand times! That would be as bad as the death of a thousand cuts.

The events that unfolded on 'sailing' day were a complete surprise to the Director of the Antarctic Division, Dr Phillip Law, the ship's captain, crew, and all the expeditioners. Only a select few of the army detachment knew about it, and of course, Dick swore them to secrecy. But, on the other hand, Sabrina's PR people had been busy: they notified radio, TV and newspapers, and the then extant Pix magazine, a keen follower of Sabrina's Australian tour. The result was a crowd of thousands making their way to Port Melbourne Dock Number Six that afternoon to glimpse Sabrina.

Dr Phillip Law was a slim, wiry man with a commanding presence. He had a shiny bald pate, compensated for by a carefully groomed goatee beard of frosty grey. His beard looked coated permanently with permafrost, a perfect image for the Director of the Antarctic Division. He blinked excessively and rapidly when speaking; confidentially, rumoured bouts of snow blindness caused this during his expeditions into the frozen interior. The whole image was carefully crafted for maximum impact and reflected the environment in which he had made his name. Although he became seasick every trip, he steadfastly insisted on accompanying the expedition every year, accompanied by his piano accordion. Propped up in the dining room, he would play for hours while the beer flowed, and the sing-alongs got more sentimental with each passing night. It helped foster formidable team spirit before the new crew arrived at their base each year. Beer was readily available, but he forbade spirits, believing that spirits frequently led to alcoholism. Hence his imprimatur was on every aspect of the expedition.

He carefully thought out all public actions to maintain the Antarctic Division's profile at its highest level to counteract the constant efforts of the Department of External Affairs bureaucrats to limit the Division's activities severely. Fortunately, at this time, he had a strong champion in his corner in the form of minister R G Casey who enthusiastically supported the concepts and aims that Phil put forward. Thanks to his support, giant steps taken, and progress accomplished in recent years. Good publicity was essential to keep the political will and ensure that funds continued to flow.

Lord Casey Nellie Law and Phil Law

The ship's send-off was carefully staged with maximum publicity in mind. Especially this year as the new expedition was to take over the American Base Wilkes built in the Geophysical Year 1957–58 and now generously handed over to the Australians fully intact. It was a magnificent coup for the Division, so everything had to be perfect to impress the dignitaries.

Magga Dan

The Magga Dan was a picture with its bright red hull and stark white superstructure. It was Tuesday the 6th of January 1959 and was sailing day. Phil Law paused at the top of the gangplank, and a glance around showed him that all was ready for the send-off. Preparations had gone smoothly in this, his tenth year as Director, and this was the payoff for surrounding himself with an outstanding team of senior operators. They had all been to the Antarctic at least once and many times for others. As a result, they knew the standards he set and acted accordingly. Yes, all looked perfect - he frowned suddenly. What was that DUKW still doing on the wharf alongside the ship? The other DUKW, was already loaded on the offside foredeck earlier this morning. Both should have been on by now, must check later, he thought.

His eyes narrowed as he surveyed the crowd arriving. Usually, only hundreds turned up to hear the speeches and watch the send-off. His Operations Officer, Frank McMahon, always put out a substantial PR blurb to all news media on the pending annual expedition about the departure schedule. My word Frank had overdone it this year as, if not mistaken, there were thousands of people there already, and more were pouring in by the minute. He thought, 'Well, I suppose, there'll be quite a few dignitaries here today; more than usual, Richard Casey, the Minister, and Lawrence (Bill) Lane, the American

Ambassador for the preliminary handover of Wilkes Base. But, the actual handover would occur at Wilkes Base, when the Magga Dan arrived. All the usual bureaucrat hangers-on from the External Affairs Department - quite the momentous occasion.' He looked at his watch; Sir William would be here anytime now, can always rely on him to be right on time. Just then, Sir William's Rolls oozed up, gently making its way through the crowd, who gave him generous applause. He was a popular Governor-General with his blunt, no-nonsense way with an outstanding war record, strongly appealed to the Australian's psyche. His wife, elegant Lady Aileen Slim, was sitting beside him.

The rostrum used for speakers was the head of the gang-plank for its raised position to look out over the crowd. It had a red carpet rolled down the gangplank for effect. In front of the gangplank on the wharf, there were comfortable seats for the visiting dignitaries. The large crowd stood around the seats, spreading up and down the wharf craning their necks for a view. They had even taken vantage points in cranes on the wharf to get a better view. Photographers swarmed around, and flashbulbs were popping at regular intervals. Visy News was there to record the event with cine cameras.

Sir William Slim

The ADC, his gold braid glistening in the sunlight, sprang from the front and hurried to open the door for Sir William and Lady Slim, smartly saluting as he did so. Phillip stepped forward to greet them and escorted them to their seats, exchanging small talk on the way. The guests, barely seated, and Phil was striding towards the gangplank when he heard the crowd roar as if they were at a football final. A siren wailed briefly. Stunned, he quickly looked around and saw two motorcycle escorts flanking an open-topped pink Cadillac coming up the dock with a stunning blonde woman in white, sitting in the back, waving, and blowing kisses to the crowd.

Eric Macklin standing behind him, muttered, 'That's Sabrina!' 'What? Who?' stammered Phil, completely stunned, 'You know Sabrina, she was at the Tivoli, and they're all ravin' about her.' 'My God! Find out what she's doing here quickly,' he said with a hasty glance down at the assembled dignitary guests, craning their heads around to see what was going on. Sweat suddenly beaded his forehead. He could see his carefully laid plans unravelling unless they could salvage the situation.

Minutes later, Eric came back with Lieutenant Dick Willing in tow. Phil eyed him suspiciously, 'What's this all about Dick?' A relaxed Dick Willing said, 'You know when we spoke the other night over beers that the expedition would wither and die if it didn't get good publicity?' 'Yeah, but so what?' 'It got me thinking. If I could get Sabrina to come along and christen my DUKW, you could not get better publicity than that! So, I asked her, and she said she would be delighted, and here she is.'

'But in God's name, why didn't you tell me?' Dick looked at him pityingly. 'Come on, Phil, you know you would have refused.' 'Er um, I'd best go with you and meet her and introduce her to the main guests.' 'Yeah,' said Dick,' I'm sure they'd love to meet her. Look at them ogling her now.'

Phil looked down at the Cadillac, surrounded by reporters with their camera's flashing and all the time yelling at Sabrina to look at them. His prominent guests were looking on in astonishment and were enjoying the show.

Minutes later, he was standing alongside the Cadillac. As Dick opened the door and helped Sabrina out through the clamouring crowd, he made a theatrical movement to introduce her, 'Sabrina, this is the Director of the Antarctic Division, Dr Phillip Law.' 'So *pulleesed* to meet you Dr, Dick has told me so much about you.' In a surprisingly well-modulated voice, no dumb blonde this person. Reluctantly wrenching his gaze from her bosom, he gallantly bowed over her hand, murmuring, 'Pleasure's all mine, Sabrina, what a wonderful surprise.' He certainly meant the surprise part.

'Before we christen the DUKW, I would like you to join the official party. Would you allow me to escort you?' 'Of course, you will be coming too, Dick?' She asked inclusively, glancing at Willing, smiling at the pair.

Together they walked the short distance to the seated dignitaries, where the men instantly sprang to their feet in eager anticipation, eyes riveted on Sabrina's greatest asset. Phil started with the Governor-General and his wife Aileen, a pretty curtsy from Sabrina to the couple. She smilingly met their enquiries while carrying on small talk about their respective small English hometowns. Phil, watching, saw that he need not have worried. Sabrina was calm and composed and had the 'star' quality that enthralled all who met her. Sir William now was animatingly talking, 'I have heard so much about you you're incredibly famous' 'You're pretty famous yourself, Sir William.' He visibly expanded, his face reddened under this smiling retort, and he was instantly under her spell.

Next, Sabrina met the American Ambassador, Laurie Lane, who held her hand for a long time and could not get his eyes above her chest to look her in the face. He was almost drooling, to the annoyance of his wife, who was watching him hawkishly. Then, finally, Minister Richard Casey, tall, slim, and elegant, shook her hand and bantered with her with a twinkle in his eye. They seemed to get along famously, which gave Phil great satisfaction. It was going well; his chagrin at her unexpected arrival evaporated. Sabrina graciously moved on to the lesser dignitaries who were almost panting in line. Meanwhile, Dick sauntered behind Phil and her with more than one set of female eyes on him speculatively. Nattily attired in his army greens, he was the perfect escort.

Phil escorted Sabrina to a seat, saying, 'I'll get Don Styles to announce the revised program. We will have your DUKW christening ceremony almost immediately before the speeches. Then, of course, you and your party will join the official group for drinks aboard the Magga later?' Sabrina smiled sweetly at him, answering in a low contralto, 'Super! I'd love to see inside a polar ship'.

After Sabrina took her seat, Don Styles, the tall Kiwi ex-pat, assumed the top of the gangplank, dragging the microphone stand towards him, leaned over, and announced: 'Honoured guests, ladies and gentlemen. The first item on the program this afternoon will be the christening of the DUKW, 'Sabrina,' on the wharf, by our star Sabrina!' A great roar and whistles from the crowd. Sabrina looked around and waved - another roar. 'Following that a welcoming speech by the Director of The Antarctic Division, Dr Phillip Law; a handover speech by the American Ambassador, Laurie Laine, a reply in acceptance by the Right Honourable Minister for External Affairs, Mr R G Casey and finally a farewell speech to this year's ANARE crew, the ship's complement and the DUKWees by Sir William Slim our esteemed Governor-General.' Polite applause for the first three, followed by warm applause for Sir William's name.

'Now Sabrina and Lieutenant Willing, if you can make your way to the DUKW on the wharf, we'll let the christening ceremony begin'. A roar and more whistles from the crowd as Sabrina and Dick left their seats. They made their way to the DUKW, where the rest of the Army detachment formed around an A-frame, rigged up by the RAEME Sergeant. From the A-frame at the end of a long rope dangled a bottle of champagne suggestively, just within swinging distance of the bow of the DUKW.

Sabrina grasped the bottle, and looking across at Dick, who was smilingly watching her, said, 'what do I do now, Richard? The photographers gathered around eagerly. One yelled out, 'swing the champagne bottle as hard as you can against the bow Sabrina, and make sure it breaks!' 'Sure, you're strong enough, Sabrina?' Another reporter yelled, 'Watch and learn. I didn't spend all those years in the gym for nothing.' As she swung the bottle hard against the DUKW, the bottle shattered into fragments and the champagne frothed and bubbled down the bow of the DUKW. With a giggle of delight, Sabrina grabbed the handheld mike and said, 'God bless this DUKW which I now name Sabrina, and God bless all who sail in her.' A mighty cheer from the crowd followed by sustained clapping as she bowed triumphantly to them.

'Now, the crane will host the DUKW onto the ship. Are you game, Sabrina?' Shouted Dick, reaching for her hand. The big forward gantry crane lowered the spider for four army crew to grasp a hook and hook them onto the four lifting points. 'Try and stop me,' she panted, grasping his hand. Then, with a flurry of skirts, she swung aboard. Her manager covered his eyes in fear.

Holding the canopy bow behind the driver's seat with her right hand, she turned and faced the crowd, waving vigorously with her left, as they hoisted the DUKW aloft with its bright gold top and standard army green hull. The adoring crowd went wild, cheering wildly, as she soared above them. Then, ever so gently, they lowered the DUKW into position on the deck. Sabrina, assisted down from the DUKW by eager ship's crew hands and wended her way along to the gangplank, where she paused theatrically for a final wave before walking down the red carpet to her seat below. Dick followed leisurely and seated himself beside her.

The speeches that followed were mercifully short and to the point as it was a hot afternoon, and they were an anti-climax after the excitement of the DUKW christening. Nevertheless, Sir William Slim's speech was a memorable one. He was a very inspiring speaker. Spontaneous applause interrupted three times. The large crowd was in a good mood and responded generously to all speeches.

When the formal part of the send-off was over, the dignitaries slowly moved up the red-carpeted gangplank to the ship's dining room and anteroom. There was a fantastic display of food laid out for the special guests. Sven, the ship's Hoffmaster, had excelled himself with his spread for the day's luncheon: fresh Tasmanian oysters in their shell, fresh lobster and Queensland mud crabs and a giant salmon as the centrepiece decorated lavishly. In addition, there was a natural live pineapple light, to the amazement of the guests. The innards scraped out of the pineapple and served separately as a tasty side dish. The pineapple skin, with the green top still attached, sat over a weak light bulb that lit up the skin's lattice-like pattern. Guests exclaimed in amazement when they realised that the pineapple skin and top were real and not a plastic copy.

The white-coated ship's stewards constantly circled with glasses of pink and white champagne on silver trays as well as white and red wines. On separate small tray mobiles strategically placed lurked the deadly Aquavit, beads of cold on the outside of each bottle flanked by the prescribed cold Tuborg beer (at eleven per cent alcohol) for the chaser. This Danish National spirit drink made from fermented potatoes was dynamite and packed a wallop that sneaks up on you. The External Affairs bureaucrats, unaware of the drink's potency, commenced to 'skol' repeatedly with first the Aquavit then the Tuborg chaser in bravado acts of sheer recklessness.

The guests thronged Sabrina wherever she moved, an old hand at these sorts of functions. She chatted pleasantly with various groups as she moved around, her champagne glass held delicately in her hand – though seldom sipped if you were an astute observer. The photographers still followed her diligently until one persistent photographer called out, 'Sabrina, will you and the Lieutenant come over here by the map of the Antarctic for a special shot.' They obliged, posing carefully with Dick smilingly pointing to Wilkes on the large map of Antarctica on the anteroom wall while Sabrina peered closely over his shoulder. Several photos later and 'perfect that will be one for the record!'

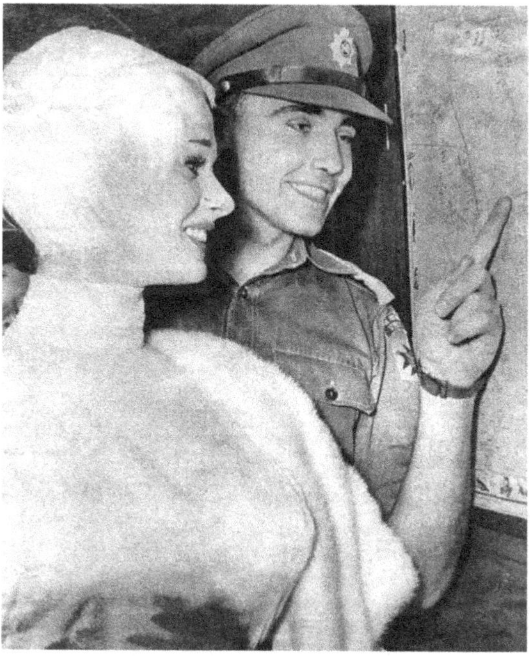

Sabrina and Dick Willing. Looking at Antarctica Map and 'Sabrina Land'

Reg, Sabrina's manager, glanced at his watch and exclaimed, 'Holy cow! Look at the time we have to rush to make your next appointment at the charity function Sabrina.' 'Oh, do we have to go, Reggie? I'm having such a super time?' Her manager was insistent. Reluctantly Sabrina made her farewells, initially to the Governor-General, who bowed over her hand, exclaiming what a pleasure it was to have met her. 'Likewise, Sir William, I have always been an admirer of yours.' Sabrina always knew the right thing to say. 'I'll come with you, Sabrina,' volunteered Phil, 'No, No, Dr, you stay with your guests, Richard will escort me' smiling at Dick, who gallantly gave her his arm.

When they appeared at the top of the gangplank again, they noted that although the crowd had thinned a little most were still waiting to get another glimpse of Sabrina; roars and whistles greeted her appearance. So, they quickly made their way to the Cadillac while the crowd gathered around, and the ever-present photographers clicked away furiously. Sabrina was always obliging to the photographers as she and the photographers had a symbiotic relationship. They both knew it; she was incredibly gracious to them, and they loved her for it.

As she climbed into the car, the V8 engine throbbed into life. Turning to Dick and holding his hand, she said severely, 'Now you will look after my DUKW Richard, no scratches or dents and treat her tenderly.' 'My lady', quoted Dick fervently, 'Sabrina will be cosseted, spoiled, and driven as if I was the Queen's chauffer.' 'Seriously, I do not know when I have had a better time, Richard. Thank you for the honour, I'll never forget it' and leaning forward, she bussed him on the cheek. The crowd whistled and clapped loudly. Touching his cheek reverently, Dick said, 'heck, I won't be able to shave there for weeks now.' 'Aren't you going to the Antarctic, and don't you wear beards down there?' Dick brightened, 'of course, right, I won't shave for at least five weeks,' reluctantly, with heavy heart, he released her hand. His heady time with the star is ending. The Cadillac eased forward; the crowd clapped and cheered as Sabrina turned to wave to them. Dick watched the Cadillac until it disappeared out of sight, then, sighing, turned and made his way back to the Magga Dan.

Sir William Slim and Dr Phillip Law were in earnest conversation in the ship's anteroom when he arrived. Sir William said, 'I always enjoy this send-off as one of the best of the calendar year; this is what my fifth time?' 'Yes, Sir William.' 'By Jove, it was a clever idea of yours getting Sabrina along. Who would have thought that a star like that could be so charming? She certainly drew the crowd.' 'I had nothing to do with her presence, although, I admit her presence gave us much needed marvellous publicity. It was Lieutenant Dick Willing here who organised it.' Turning to Dick as he spoke. 'Was it you, Mr Willing, how on earth? – no, don't answer that! Seriously it was a PR trump card, and you deserve commendation for it –I must speak to the CGS about it.' Dick said nothing, standing, smilingly in front of the Governor-General, slightly embarrassed but presenting a calm exterior.

'When did you graduate? Duntroon, I presume?'

'Yes, sir. You reviewed my passing out parade in December '57.'

'Well, you've certainly made a good start, showing the elan you did today, great stuff!'

Glancing sideways at his wife Aileen, who was in an animated conversation with Mrs Casey and the American Ambassador's wife, he said, 'well, dear, it's time we left this delightful party and let the crew relax.' Offering her his arm as he spoke.

Don Styles called attention to the assemblage that the Governor-General was leaving, and the guests stood politely and gave him a round of applause; saluting them, he turned and walked up the steps with his entourage. Phillip accompanied him down the gangplank to the shiny black Rolls, where the ADC held the door open, saluting him as he and his wife settled themselves. Sir William poked his head out the window for the last word, 'Wonderful day, Phil, keep it up.' 'I will, sir, I will!'

There was applause as the Rolls drove off from the very much reduced crowd that had now primarily melted away with the departure of Sabrina leaving. After that, only friends and relatives of the expeditioners said their last goodbyes.

With the departure of the Governor-General, the rest of the official party soon left. Eric Macklin and Doug Twigg supported the legless External Affairs bureaucrats to their white Commonwealth hire car to take them to the airport.

The shadows lengthened, all traces of the party over, the ship's crew readied for departure. Soon the ship's engine throbbed into life, 'cast-off forward, cast-off aft', a tug nudged and manoeuvred the ship away from the wharf and turned it to head down the Yarra and out into the bay. Final yells and waves across the water, tears from wives and girlfriends, frantic waving of the children and lumps in throats of the expeditioners leaving their loved ones for thirteen months.

The little red hulled ship gathered speed, its seven-cylinder engine pounding. It would attain and maintain an average speed of around ten knots for a journey of nine to ten thousand miles before returning in several weeks. Next, in about eight to ten days would come the excitement of seeing the first icebergs followed in a couple of days by the eerie silence of the icepack, breakthrough in three or five days if they were lucky. The ice pack surrounding Wilkes Base can be very unpredictable (the 1966/7 voyage of the Nella Dan saw it stuck fast for twenty-eight days). Finally, after the pack, the rocky, icy mainland and the red huts of Wilkes Base – destination achieved.

'Yes, Vin, he just rang me to say he wished to commend young Lt Willing for his initiative in getting Sabrina to name a DUKW after her as it brought tremendously good publicity to the Antarctic Division.'

'Good publicity?'

'Yes, indeed, and from the reports I have seen, it is good publicity for the Army too, don't you think?'

'Eh, yes, sir.'

'The DUKW was probably only going to be named after some old fogie anyway, wasn't it?'

'Yes, probably, sir.'

'Well, I'd watch that young man if I were you – the Army needs people with such dash – pass on my commendations to him, will you.'

'Yes, I will certainly watch him, sir!'

'Thanks, Vin. Nice to pass on good news for a change. Keep up the excellent work, goodbye.'

'Uh, goodbye, sir.'

Hanging up the phone, Dowdy, totally bemused, tried to take it in, 'verbal commendation from the Governor-General, excellent publicity for the Army?' He sighed and thought, *what the heck, guess I can't stay mad at him after that. Guess I'd best say nothing and just act as if nothing happened when he returns. Commendation? I do not think so! But, if I did that, what would he get up to next?*

Sadly, Major R.T. Willing MBE passed away in his sleep on the 8th of August 2008 in Maleny, Qld. A comet who roared across our skies, others were lucky enough to be sprinkled with cosmic dust as he passed. I consider it a privilege to have known him. God bless you. Dick.

THE ACTION OF A BORN SURVIVOR

Dear Diary:

Today is the 16th of January 1966 – locstat (location status) Wilkes Base Antarctica. It was the former American base, established for the Geophysical year 1958 and handed over to the Australians for their use. The red/orange buildings, now all covered with snow and ice, and the base, they say, is deteriorating rapidly. Three days ago, I arrived on the 'Nella Dan', A. J. Lauritzen Lines Polar Ship. So far, all unloading has gone very smoothly, and both DUKWS (the six-wheeled drive amphibians made famous during the second world war) are performing well.

I am mightily impressed with the ice ramp entrance to the base from the bay. Ice walls about twenty feet high and a smooth ramp all the way – Ted Love, last year's DUKW boss, said we may need chains to exit each day, but so far, no such problems.

At the end of each summer, the expeditioners lay explosives on the ramp floor and blow it up at the start of the following summer before bulldozing out the ice and reforming the ramp. If the weather heats up, the ice base begins to melt, and the rivulets of water running down the ramp causes jagged edges, which can puncture the tyres, or the ramp can become boggy; that is why they may need chains. We have been fortunate as the weather has remained stable between eighteen- and thirty-degrees Fahrenheit, so no melt.

The bay is breathtaking, with the ink-blue sea dotted with 'bergy bits' (small pieces broken off larger icebergs). They can be as small as a little car or as large as a bus which will linger until they join up again in the winter when the sea freezes again. They are mainly Gentoo penguins around this location; some perched on the bergy bits, and others swimming around our DUKWS like schools of porpoises, crazy critters who virtually fly under the water and sometimes take enormous forty-foot leaps out of the water as they build up speed alongside us (up to eighteen knots), I have been told.

The Yanks certainly built themselves a comfortable base, considering it was only supposed to last for a year. They also have goodies, films, and a modern projector; they have a turn-table and disc jockey set-up with transmitting mike and heaps of vinyl records (thirty-three rpm extended plays). Some of the 1964/65 expeditioners here and I are already planning a disc jockey request session for the boys on the Thala Dan, who expect to be bored witless while the Thala crunches its way through the ice pack next week. Bob Colson and his crew are on board, so I must get a special welcome for the 'Duckies' up and running. We are currently working up the advertisements; I am plugging one for the green and yellow cabs (our DUKWS). Ken Bennet's homebrew gets a guernsey (KB lager, of course) and Mick's clothing store 'Muk Luks specials (like Ugg boots) in the latest fashion straight from Greenland' – we will need them and others to keep the disc jockey's patter rolling along smoothly.

You have got to love the huskies, chained together out on the snow, where they make little air pockets and let the snow cover them—chained within a snarling distance of each other as they would rip one another's throats out, given no provocation at all. One of the dog sledders here said they are vicious with each other but very gentle with their handlers. He said he has stepped between fighting dogs slashing at each other and when they feel they have his hand in their mouth by accident, they let go instantly, and he said their mouth never even breaks the skin. Don't think I would like to try out his theory myself.

The dogs are extremely smart, and they often outfox the penguins, who are dumb, really. The penguins roost inland at night but must pass close to the circle of chained dogs to get to the sea each day. Penguins always travel in a lengthy line, one behind each other, so much so that on coming into the base, I saw long black lines snaking up from the sea and was surprised to learn that they were penguins heading inland. Also, they ignore the dogs who fancy them as a change of diet from their monotonous diet of seal meat each day.

The penguin line would snake its way within feet of the dog's chained circle, with the dogs straining at the end of their chains to get at them, barking and slavering at the tasty morsels only feet away. The penguins ignored them insouciantly, waddling their way towards the sea, keeping the same distance always from the straining dogs. 'Aha', thought the dogs, 'we can work together on this', so while one dog strained at the end of his chain, the one alongside him crouched right back on his chain waiting until the penguin line swerved in keeping the necessary few feet away from where he crouched then 'wham' change of diet, shared with his mate. The guys here said the penguins never learn of the deception and fall for it frequently.

The Nella Dan has two missions this trip. Firstly to offload stores for the Wilkes' Base (mail, beer and other essential items - about 10 tons worth). Then offload about 200 tons of building supplies for the new REPSTAT (Resupply Station) under construction. After the Nella Dan completes that, the Mawson expeditioners will begin construction of the new station for a couple of weeks before Phase Two. Phase Two is to sail a couple of thousand miles around the coastline to Mawson Base to unload 650 tons there and change over the Mawson expedition crews. The Thala Dan, on the way in next week , will have about 750 tons to unload for the Wilkes' Base.

REPSTAT is on a bleak rock-strewn ridge running down into the bay about two miles across the bay, from Wilkes Base. The wind howls across this ridge all the time, rarely less than twenty knots, and it is not the most pleasant of places. However, Eric Macklin, the expedition Operations Officer I work for, explained that the ridge was chosen deliberately, as the wind kept the snow clean from it to leave the bare rock for most of the year-round.

Boy, there will be a constant 'banshee' howl around the base buildings when completed. From the plans, the base will consist of a long series of interconnected structures, some 200 yards long of a monotonous grey colour running down the ridgeline– compared to the bright orange/red of the snow-covered Wilkes where we are now.

Unloading had been routine so far, that was until today's incident. My knees are still knocking together when I think of how close my two DUKW crew and I came to being blown sky-high – our survival chances were absolutely zilch, zero if the diesel had ignited. I must secretly admire Director Sir Phillip Law, demonstrating that he is a 'born survivor' and a 'low-risk taker' during an emergency.

It is not hard to admire Dr Phillip, the current director of ANARE (Australian National Antarctic Research Expedition).

As the director for around thirty years, his singular drive and verve have allowed Australia to punch well above its weight in the Antarctic stakes. As I saw today, his ability to 'minimise risk' has preserved him to take a position of eminence within the division and the Australian folklore of the Antarctic, only surpassed by the great Sir Douglas Mawson.

We were all incredibly impressed when Dr Phillip first walked into the lecture room to address the expeditioners on our weeklong pre-embarkation course. Here was this legend coming to address us! Aesthetically slim, a baldpate, compensated for by a carefully cultivated and neatly trimmed beard, suitably frosted with grey to give the impression to the observer of 'Permafrost' settling on his beard. He had almost non-existent eyebrows and a habit of blinking rapidly and continuously. One of my colleagues told me in an awed voice, resulting from his periods of snow blindness suffered during his treks out over the blinding white icescape that is the Antarctic norm. Who could not be impressed? On talking with him later, I noted a man of great intellect, interested in the classics, and fascinated with Chinese Checkers of all things.

Taken all in all, Dr Phillip Law was an admirable man and fondly and confidently looked up to by all expedition members, especially and including the ship's captain and crew. J Lauritzen Lines, the Danish Company from which the Australian Antarctic Division chartered the two polar ships used each year for about three months, each at one thousand pounds per day. They thought so much of him that they named the ship we sailed in 'Nella Dan', after his wife, Nellie Law. Her framed photograph smiled down on us from the dining room wall each night at dinner. However, I swear that I saw the smile turn to a frown during the New Year's Eve celebrations this year when I had drunk too much akvavit (the deadly highly alcoholic Danish distilled spirit) and skolled too much beer.

As I said, an impressive leader with impeccable credentials, fearless, brave, and mainly 'intrepid', the 'in word' for all expeditioners, so today came as a bit of a shock to me.

The day started simply enough; we unloaded the Nella Dan from the forward hatch into the two DUKWs. Each DUKW had three crew members, a driver and two loaders to assist – these loaders were not army personnel but assigned to us from the expeditioners. Usually, they stayed with us for the duration of the voyage. They preferred an orderly system employed on the DUKWs to the chaos of the expeditioners ashore in trying to sort out the supplies as they arrived.

The DUKWs are painted yellow non-slip paint on the top for safety and the standard army green on the bottom. The bright yellow top was a concession made to DUKWs operating in the Antarctic for easier recognition in the rougher seas. The Nella Dan employed a twenty-five-ton capacity crane on the forward hatch, and usually, we received loads in large cargo nets lowered over the side. The crane then manoeuvred the loads into position, and the cargo nets returned to the ship after unloading them ashore.

For unloading drums, they used a spider attached to the crane. It was a strong steel ring fitting over the crane hook with four lengths of steel wire rope, braided and reinforced onto the ring with small L-shaped hooks. These fitted snugly into the rim of the forty-four-gallon drum on the end of each eight-foot rope. The drums offloaded in pairs while the DUKW crew danced gingerly around the cargo hull edges. Finally, they manoeuvred them into position before releasing the hooks and sending the spider aloft for the next pair of drums. The system was well-tried and efficient; we could load a DUKW with twenty-six drums in about twenty minutes.

The 1942 handbook (year of manufacture of the DUKWs) gave the maximum load capacity at around sixteen forty-four-gallon drums. Still, of course, we ignored such trivialities as 'a safe guide', preferring to take as many as we could to speed up the unloading. As a result, the two DUKWs operated in a rotating fashion, one usually ashore unloading at REPSTAT, about a mile over the icy water from the ship, while the other DUKW was snug alongside the Nella Dan taking on a load. The unloading was thus fluent, continuous, and rapid.

The scene that morning was picture perfect: the Nella Dan with its white superstructure and bright red body was one of the famed 'red polar ships' of the J. Lauritzen lines. The ships were painted bright red for ease of finding by their deck helicopters returning across vast distances in the white wastelands of Greenland and Antarctica, where they operated year-round. The red ship contrasted sharply with the ink-blue sea and the white bergy bits floating in the bay. On a tiny bergy bit just in front of the ship's bow, two Gentoo penguins in their formal evening wear perched unconcernedly, watching as the flurry of unloading continued around them. In the distance across the bay, the blue ice cliffs rose from the water, and the icy white landscape shone stark and bright beyond them.

I approached the ship's port side under the forward end, at the recommended approach angle of about twenty-five degrees. Before contacting the black 'sausage' (a large inflatable rubber bladder about twenty feet long, tied alongside the ship to prevent damage to the DUKW as the ship rose and fell with the waves during unloading), I swung the wheel hard away from the ship. I revved the engine vigorously to give the DUKWS a quick thrust to bring the rear end hard against the sausage before tying up and beginning to take on our next load. It was mid-morning, and we were alongside for our fourth load of the day. Things were going smoothly indeed, which should have been warning enough.

Twenty minutes later, we had taken on twenty-four drums when the final two drums came over the side, one of them leaking badly from a dent in its side. Eric Macklin called out to me from the deck above, 'just take that leaking drum out to the middle, put a hole in it with your axe, and throw it over the side, please, Jim.' 'Yeah, okay,' I shouted back.

We released the DUKW from the ship's hook, and I swung the wheel over, revved up the engine smartly, engaged the prop and headed towards the two metal guideposts which marked the egress from the water to REPSTAT. I disengaged the prop about 200 yards from the ship and crawled onto the DUKW's bow, where I retrieved the axe from its bracket.

The leaking drum was in the middle of the cargo hold, and there were two drums beneath it, so aiming, I launched many powerful chops into the lid, causing the diesel to spray and drip furiously down into the hold of the DUKW. Now, although I had put the prop shaft gear lever into neutral to stop the propeller from spinning while we remained motionless on the water, the prop shaft itself continued to spin over. It turned out to be almost disastrous because, on the second blow from the axe, the thin metal rim holding up the boards in the cargo hold floor bent, and the large floorboard, about six by four feet, collapsed onto the revolving prop shaft, sparks flew. Within minutes, we had flames licking up from the cargo hold floor within mere inches of the dripping diesel.

Dropping the axe like it was a red-hot poker, I raced for the Very pistol under the driver's seat. Now we had two cartridges for the Very pistol, red for HELP WANTED NOW and green for 'Could you give us a hand when you're ready please'. The pistol always loaded with a red Very cartridge, as we figured you always had enough time to load a green cartridge if you needed a green one. Not so with a red cartridge. This situation called for a red Very flare.

So, pointing the pistol skywards, I pulled the trigger and watched as the flare arced out over the sea. Meanwhile, Chris and Ned, my crew members, watched in horror as the flames licked higher and higher.

Wait, instant help was at hand, practically saved, as on the water now was Dr Phil and a crew member in the big MacRobertson Miller launch (the launch was a donation from the chocolate people) its powerful Volvo engine snarling as the launch swooped and cavorted around in front of the Nella Dan. Seeing the flare, Dr Phil elegantly heeled over the launch and headed towards us with a rooster tail of frothy water behind. 'Thank god' was our collective mutter. Hello, what is this? The launch suddenly stopped fifty yards from the stricken DUKW, with the bow almost dipping into the water.

Dr Phil, with cupped hands, yelled across the water. 'What's the problem?' I yelled back, 'we've got a fire.' 'What have you got on board?' 'Uh, twelve drums of diesel and fourteen drums of gasoline.'

Dr Phil disappeared behind the Perspex, and suddenly, the Volvo engine roared wildly as the launch made a 180-degree turn and, with a four-foot-high rooster tail trailing in its wake, hared out across the bay away from us as fast as it could go.

'Wadda we do now?' moaned Ned as stricken we watched the fast-disappearing launch. As one, we turned to look at the flames now licking close to the dripping diesel. The only way I could stop the fire was to stop the propeller shaft rotating and then douse the fire with our two big red CO2 fired extinguishers on board. Using the fire extinguishers before stopping the shaft turning was useless, as the fire would promptly ignite again. So, thinking I raced to the driver's seat and turned off the motor, shaft stopped – 'now douse it!' I yelled to Ned and Chris, who were on standby with the fire extinguishers at the ready – SQUIRT, SQUIRT, SQUIRT. A white cloud quickly turned to foam, and the fire was out – we started breathing again.

We all then heaved and pulled the leaking drum upright and, with one last mighty heave, threw it overboard where it swirled towards the bottom 200 feet below to lie there and ooze its deadly cargo into the pristine blue water above.

I casually picked up the Very pistol, loaded a green flare, and fired it into the air. Moments later, the other DUKW cruised over to us to see what the matter was. I explained that we could not start the engine until we were ashore, and they would have to tow us in. But, unfortunately, to do this, a rope tow would be useless. So, the only solution was to hook the big chain on the DUKW's bow over the Pintle hook on the rear of the towing DUKW. The only problem now was, said Pintle hook was about two feet underwater, and the water was only water and not ice because of its salt content.

I looked hopefully at the crew on the other DUKW, but they just stared back at me with arms resolutely folded. Then, sighing, I thought being the boss sucked sometimes and began to strip off. First, removing the RFD life jacket, then my submarine jacket, followed by my overalls, my red ANARE jumper, my blue RAAF pyjama top and finally, my long-sleeved skivvy to leave me standing bared and shivering in the decidedly brisk air.

The Pintle hook had a retaining pin, requiring considerable force and wiggling to get it out before opening the hook. I could only bear the cold for about two minutes at a time before I had to come up for a breather. Then, after much wiggling and 'oohing and aahing,' the pin finally released, and I was able to open the towing hook, quickly slam the heavy chain in place, shut the top of the hook and force the retaining pin back home. After which, gasping, I came up for air and a frantic hop around the deck, rubbing myself down vigorously, my teeth chattering while I tried to get the circulation going again in my blue coloured upper body. The other DUKW crew, Ned and Chris, thought it was hilarious.

The rest of the recovery was routine, and a half-hour later, we were back receiving loads from the ship as if nothing had happened.

Mystified why our 'hero' had so ruthlessly abandoned us in our dire time of need, it only occurred later to me why Sir Phillip took such dramatic action. Being so busy with our crisis, Ned, Chris, and I did not realise the gravity of our situation, for if the diesel had ignited, the much more volatile petroleum drums would quickly have exploded. Fourteen drums of petroleum would have made a spectacular bang – anyone within 100 yards of the DUKW would have blown sky-high.

Dr Phil, of course, had ascertained the situation immediately and taken the right and proper course of a truly born survivor. My knees knock together now when I think of our close shave, but you must admire him; swift, decisive action minimising the risk to himself. Us on the DUKW? A small matter of collateral damage if the drums exploded, that was all. Funny, it seemed that Dr Phil avoided me for the rest of the day; then again, I was just paranoid about it, and it was my imagination running riot.

Ho Hum Diary, we will see what tomorrow brings –I am beginning to see why they have coined the word 'intrepid' for activities down here,

THE GAME

From Lieutenant Colonel Jim Doohan (RL)
Kyogle, NSW

To Lieutenant Colonel John Tracey (RL)
Canberra ACT.

Dear John,

After fifty years, you need an explanation why the sigs rugby team attacked me so much after halftime when you and the rest of the team came to my rescue. I hope this clears up a few matters and must apologize for my actions - though might I say you did a terrific job that day. The story goes something like the following, and the severity of my punishment can be explained by a few other incidents – including the fire in the paludrine bowl, which you, of course, knew about:

Paul Flanagan, a white can of Fosters draught in his hand, sipped reflectively and started talking enthusiastically about the football field we would be playing on against the sig squadron rugby team that afternoon.

'You ought to see it, Jim, the field's rough as guts, it's in the middle of the police cadet academy, and I tell you, you watch where you step. Yeah, keep your eyes on the ground, mate, or else you could put your foot into a stinker. Those cadets aren't too particular where they go to the toilet'.

I listened, open-mouthed; I had played rugby on ropey pitches before – including the Nimbin showground where I nearly drowned. I was sixteen and the lock forward for the Kyogle Wallaroos playing against Nimbin (before the arrival of the 'Flower Power' people) and the so-called team's 'gun tackler'. Half the team yelled at me near the end of the game, 'quick, Jim tackle Jingles, quick!' Jingles was a nineteen stone Nimbin prop who was now rumbling towards the try line in the southwestern corner with the ball tucked under his arm. I was ten stone wringing wet those days, and the only way I could 'cut 'em down' was a scything tackle around the ankles. Trouble was on this day, we had just endured a terrific downpour during the match, and the corner where he was heading was under three feet of water. So, when I hit him, he had such momentum that we slid about five yards right into the water with me underneath. Jingles lay on top of me, moaning but not moving. I squirmed, wriggled, and gagged; only my teammates saved me by just managing to drag me out in time, spluttering, coughing, and retching, seconds before I succumbed. Now that was a field to remember! Nevertheless, this field sounded infinitely worse, long grass, rocks and brownies scattered liberally in this sweltering heat; this match was going to be a stinker!

So we went; the pitch was about as rough as Paul had described it. I warily scanned it for 'brown jobs' but fortunately saw none. However, before the match had started, we had a peek at the cadet's quarters. 'Look at their pillows', exclaimed John Tracey pointing towards a lump of wood. 'A pillow, you must be joking?' But a pillow it was, and worse, their beds were just bare boards! Man, these guys sure do it tough.

It was around halftime, and we were in strife, and the 'strife' boiled down to the large, fast hip swivelling Kiwi centre in the sigs team. Who, I reckon, trained with the All Blacks. With his hip swivelling, swerving, jinking run, the attempted tacklers slid off him like they were trying to grab a greasy pig, and he had already effortlessly run in three tries.

Finally, I could stand it no longer, 'leave him to me,' I screamed as he once again began his devastating run for the line and towards me. I lined him up carefully and crunch-tackled him. I grabbed a handful of family jewels as he went down and squeezed extra hard!

'Ooooh, sir!' He shrilled in a high-pitched falsetto voice with the ball rolling free from his convulsive grasp. 'Tweet! Knock on,' yelled Winifred Fowles, the referee, and we had the ball feed and won the ball from the scrum. We made good progress up the field until Paul was forced into touch just as the whistle blew halftime. My teammates were blissfully unaware of my inexcusable (though effective action).

I secretly watched the sigs team during the halftime break. The Kiwi was talking vocally and loudly and waving his arms around. From where I was, I could hear loud mutterings and growls and threats rumbling across the field as scores of pairs of eyes searched me out.

Halftime over, the sigs team trotted out onto the field led by Sgt Blue – a giant redhead with arms swinging akimbo. As he came onto the field, he snuffled and growled with his piggy little eyes fixed on me like burning coals.

Sigs team kicked off to us, and foolishly I took the ball – then, all hell broke loose. Blue hit me with a pile driver tackle with his teeth snapping dangerously close to my ear. Instantly the rest of the sigs' forwards rushed in, yelling like fiends attempting to kick me and jump on me while I curled up in the foetal position as near as I could get. Blue has now straddled me with a red fist held aloft, ready to pound me again. Meanwhile, with a combined yell of rage at this 'unsportsmanlike' behaviour, my team heroically ran into the fray to my rescue, kicking, punching, and gouging happily. But, of course, good old John Tracey was right there, fists and legs pumping like a thrashing machine.

Underneath it all, curled up as I was, I could see the side of Sgt Blue's jaw exposed enticingly. I jabbed a six-inch cat's paw at it with the last of my strength with my right hand.

Blue groaned and rolled over dead out to it, to my astonishment. To this day, I do not know if it was my cat's paw jab or someone else like John Tracey slugging him with a rabbit killer. Down the bottom of the ruck, as I was, it was impossible to tell.

The sigs champion, Sgt Blue, needed carrying off, head lolling sideways, and at this, the sigs supporters and team let out a banshee-like howl of fury and ran at us again, ripping and tearing. Poor old Win Fowles stood on the edge of the melee furiously blowing his whistle until we wondered if the pea would disintegrate. Then, after about ten minutes together with growls and muttered threats, the football game finally restarted.

Interestingly, the Vietnamese Police Cadets, who had numbered a scarce half dozen disinterested spectators in the first half of the game, had now swelled to one hundred or so enthusiastic viewers clapping and cheering as the fight ebbed and flowed.

Another twenty minutes passed, and the game hung in the balance. Paul Flanagan had scored on the wing, and John Tracey had scored two nippy tries from his position as breakaway, showing great strength to crash over the try line each time with three sigs tacklers clinging to him.

Their main strike weapon, the big Kiwi, was rendered entirely useless. Every time he saw me coming at him when he had the ball, he threw it wildly over his shoulder, whether there was support there or not. We were three tries and one goal apiece, and with fifteen minutes to go, their winger, a fast and solid player, had the ball and was running towards our fullback, lanky, lean, and mean Makka.

Iain McKinley was his name. He was a Victorian Nasho and a top-flight Aussie Rules player who could catch anything kicked to him and punt from one end of the field to the other. But he could not tackle to save himself, so as the winger ran towards him, we knew that just one side step and Iain would be left stranded, and a certain try under the posts was looming. So that's it, game over. However, Makka had other considerable talents, reputed to be something like Victoria's amateur welterweight champion boxer and man, could he 'go the knuckle!' All Makka could do as fullback for the entire game was watch the fights going on from one end of the field to the other with hands-on-hips and licking his lips in disappointment that he could not join the fray. Now here was his chance! As the winger bore down on him, Makka, instead of trying to tackle him, took one step towards him and 'thunk', he floored him with the most terrific uppercut I had ever seen. The winger, nearly knocked out of his boots by the force of the blow, flew backwards, landing flat on his back. The ball rolled over the sideline and out of play. The winger lay motionless while Makka flashed us a pleased smile while we stood and watched in awe. The sigs team whined with fury and ran towards Makka, howling with rage. With a yelp, the rest of us raced over to help our new champion. The brawl that followed left the other dustups as minor skirmishes as the two teams tore into each other.

The Vietnamese cadet onlookers had now swelled to about three hundred, and they were almost hysterical in their enjoyment of the spectacle, cheering wildly with every punch thrown. Unable to restrain themselves, some of the sigs' supporters ran onto the field to join in the melee. Win's whistle shrilled and shrilled, and finally, he gave up – MATCH ABANDONED.

Oh, s---t, not Major Des? Yeah, that's him all right, the same pose, knuckles clasped on knees, back ramrod straight, toothbrush moustache twitching angrily, while he stared out under the brim of his green hat. Funny, only Major Des could make a jungle green floppy hat a thing of regimental rigour; somehow, it didn't sag or flap on him but sat squarely to attention on top of his head. His gimlet eyes, now riveted on me, face flushed and angry, and of course, he just had to be the OC (Officer Commanding) of the sig squadron. *He would remember 'The Glen Incident' well,* I thought.

Meanwhile, the sig team members were milling around him and gesturing with considerable animation in my direction. I hunched my shoulders and went into 'grey mode' to make as tiny a target as possible while I slunk around the back of the team and painfully limped towards my Land Rover parked on the other side of the oval.

Yeah, it was bad timing to go up in front of the colonel. All and sundry cheekily knew him as 'Goffer King,' for his habit of sweeping the ALSG area majestically in his glossily painted Land Rover. Then he would ring the relevant unit's OCs after his patrol to give them a ticking off about the number of 'goffer cans' or soft drink cans he had seen scattered around their area of responsibility. Of course, unit OCs trembled in terror of such a phone call - of course, the rest of us knew him as 'the Goffer King'.

No, my timing was atrocious. It was less than a week after my last appearance – trivial matter really – just an exuberant celebration in the Officer's Mess for the birth of Davey Mills daughter back in Australia. I do not remember exactly how it started; except I saw Captain Davey Mills (RAE) looking very miserable in the anteroom straight after the evening meal. Usually, a top bloke with a very cheery disposition, I walked over to him and asked what was wrong. 'My wife's just had a baby daughter, and I'm over here,' Davey answered miserably.

'Bloody hell, Davey. Congratulations!' I exclaimed. 'This calls for a celebration,' and signalled to the barman to fetch me a big box of white owl cigars and a magnum of champagne. Just then, the rest of the annex patrons were starting to settle into their armchairs for the start of the Jane Fonda movie, 'They shoot horses, don't they?'

'Damn, this cork is sure hard to get out,' I exclaimed. I inadvertently pointed the mouth of the bottle towards the screen, vigorously shaking the bottle in the process. After panting and gasping, a loud 'pop' and the cork whizzed over the top of the patron's heads to smack into the screen – Davey and I laughed uproariously. We splashed what contents remained in the bottle into our glasses. An extensive trail of froth appeared on top of the bar, which the barman dabbed at furtively as we lit up our cigars and guzzled down the bubbly.

By then, Davey had brightened considerably and ordered another magnum despite the senior officers' withering glances. 'Pop!' another cork, another splat on the screen. This time, the cork whistled perilously close to the patrons' heads but triumphantly hit Fonda on her left nipple. What a wonderful time we were having. Bottle followed bottle, and apart from the corks and ribald, all would have been well if I hadn't made a terrible mistake at this time. The big fat white owl cigar, now smoked down to its butt, needed stumping out, so I carelessly reached around to the ashtray on the bar and proceeded to stump it out vigorously.

The big problem was, it wasn't the ashtray I was stumping it out in; no, it was the paludrine tablet bowl. The bowl, heaped with paludrine tablets covered in waxy paper, which I can assure you is highly flammable. 'Arghhh. Fire!' screamed the barman as he backed into the corner of the bar. I looked casually around, and do you know what, he was right? Flames were leaping two feet out of the paludrine bowl, and dense black smoke made the area uneasy.

'Yeah,' screamed Davey triumphantly, showing his engineer training; he grabbed an unopened magnum from the bar in front of us and, with a twist of his wrist, removed the cork, shook the bottle hard and proceeded to spray the fire. He also squirted the paludrine tablets burnt wax paper, and the barman crouched in terror in the corner of the bar. Finally, the fire was conclusively and effectively out; but there were bits of burned paper over the entire bar stock and the barman. A very thick black cloud of smoke was gathering near the ceiling of the annex, and the wax paper burnt with a formidable acrid smell, which permeated the whole annex. Soon, the movie patrons were coughing and spluttering and rushing for the door - Movie abandoned. The mess sergeant hastened to the barman's aid and led him whimpering away to his quarters – Bar closed. Surprisingly, Davey and I were reprimanded before the Goffer King the next day, and several duty officers handed out between us. So, my timing for this second intransigence was appalling. Though geez, the other night, I was only trying to cheer poor little Davey up.

So, I could hear it now, 'Sir, Sir Capt Doohan is a bully and blah, blah, blah…' Of course, the Goffer King was not happy to hear this, especially after my accident with the paludrine tablet bowl. Yeah, I thought that 'riot incident' was a near run thing. Thank God for poor ol' 2Lt Veasey now studying to be a doctor somewhere in Tassie; it appears the Army didn't want him, but he sure stood by me when it counted!

Funny how things all start kind of innocently and grow as they go. We were sitting in our rudely constructed Mess tent at the Glen in Shoalwater Bay in the riot case. As I recall, it was chilly, so we had pushed a great ironbark log through the side of the forty by twenty tent and lit the front half of it. We sat on the other half and contemplated the sparks darting towards the roof of the tent while we swigged on our XXXX cans and gossiped about nothing in general. After a hard, sweaty day, it was good to undertake a bit of beer-swilling and character assassination as the night wore on.

It was around 2130 hrs, and all was well, we thought, until suddenly the guard commander, a corporal, burst unceremoniously into the tent. 'Sir, sir, come quick, there's a bloody great riot going on up the hill; some big guy is beating up all the medics!'

Wow, this is what we need action! Jumping to our feet as one, we took the last swig of our cans and hurried out after the corporal, who was quickly scampering up the hill with knees bent. Me eagerness itself, failed to note at the time that as we strode towards the melee, my fellow officers slowed gradually, and we strung out rather than travel in a formidable group. Some even dropped off the end until I arrived at the fight scene, accompanied by only one other officer, 2Lt Veasey.

At the scene, I beheld a sight of absolute devastation. A giant blond soldier with bloodied knuckles stood amid a pile of medic bodies, lying in various states of disarray and displaying all sorts of cuts and bruises, all bleeding profusely and moaning pitifully.

Before the blond demolisher was a medical Warrant Officer shaking his fist in the face of the thug, I saw right away that he was about to become the next casualty. The Lance Bombardier, standing just behind the blond, was singing out, 'Go on, Luey, slug him too. He can't hurt you.'

'Right, what the bloody hell is going on here?' I roared in my best parade ground voice.

The Lance Bombardier swung around at me and sneered, 'you'll be next, you strutting, big red-headed bastard'.

I could see that this called for an immediate fix, but I would not tackle big Luey. No, takeout the brains, I reasoned, and the Frankenstein Monster would cease to function.

Without thinking about it further, I crash tackled the Lance Bombardier, and as he was down, remembering his sneering face. I soaked him a good few times to keep him passive.

Luey stood by awkwardly, rocking from foot to foot like a giant machine with the power switched off. The Lance Bombardier now looked sick. A cry went up from five or six of his drunken headquarter cronies, who had been cheering Luey on, 'we saw that officer hit that soldier!' Then, a comforting roar came from the throats of the ten or fifteen medics present, 'we didn't see a fucking thing!'

By now, the guard commander had rounded up the rest of the guard. Luey and his Lance Bombardier had been marched off to the lock-up for the night, looking subdued and tractable.

The next day Major Des, as the OC of 3 Task Force Maintenance Area (3TFMA), was officiating at the Orderly Room in which the Lance Bombardier was having his charge heard for his part in the brawl the night before. As a result, the medic Warrant Officer charged Lance Bombardier for disorderly conduct, amongst other things.

'Would I care to give evidence?' asked Major Des as 2Lt Veasey and I stood before him. 'I'll say,' I said enthusiastically and began to recount the incident of the night before as I saw it. (Of course, omitting my part in alleviating it).

Suddenly, the accused turned and looked at me from lowered brows in a whining tone, 'this officer punched me, sir.' Major Des' toothbrush moustache twitched vigorously.

'Aha,' he thought. Then in his very sternest voice, 'Is that right, CAPTAIN DOOHAN?'

'No, sir,' I lied glibly. 'He fell, and when I helped him up, he accused me of hitting him.' 'IS THAT TRUE, LT VEASEY?' thundered Major Des as he gazed sternly at 2Lt Veasey.

A tall thin chap was 2Lt Veasey, with Clark Kent glasses and a long neck with a prominent Adam's apple, which bobbed up and down several times before he answered in a hesitant, quiet voice, 'ye -yes sir'.

'Good on you, mate,' I thought. 'Right, that will be all gentlemen,' Maj Des said brusquely. He knew I had lied, but he could do naught about it.

As we walked out of the orderly room, we noted that about five or six of the Lance Bombardier's cronies were in line to say I had hit him. But – standing in a long line was about eight or ten medics to say that I hadn't hit him, bless them. So, as I walked past, I winked at them.

But damn it, as they say, what goes around comes around, and Maj Des would now have his day, delayed by nine months as it was.

Well, John, as you know, it happened just as I imagined. As I had suspected, the Goffer King, well-briefed by Major Des, read me the riot act and banned me from playing rugby again while in the country. He would have banned me for life if he could've. I received quite a few extra duties, duty officers and my favourite hate, Defending Officer, at three upcoming Court Martials. So, overall, it was a right royal bollocking.

Still, John, as I said, I sure appreciated your enthusiastic help all those years ago.

Sincerely

Jim Doohan

THE SEQUEL

Every major event has a sequel or a Newtonian third law of 'For every action, there is an equal and opposite reaction'.

In the case of my actions in the game, Karma quickly caught up with me. Almost immediately, as I was appointed Defending Officer for an upcoming Court Martial.

It was not just any Court Martial, as the defendant had drugs in his possession when caught, LSD and marijuana. In 1970, drugs were viewed very dimly by the powers to be. Inevitably, that meant the defendant would receive an automatic two-year detention - open and shut case.

Of course, I protested loudly and vociferously at my appointment. I proclaimed to all and sundry, and particularly the Court Martial Appointing Staff, that it would be most unfair, as I had an absolute hatred of the use of drugs. Thus, my appointment would be catastrophic to the poor misguided, obviously guilty miscreant.

Result? Nothing. The headquarters staff to whom I was abjectly pleading my cause were as immovable as the giant Buddha in Afghanistan. They just provided me with the details of the soldier involved, his unit and the contact officer I used to find the prisoner.

Oh, those HQ Staff, they were beauties. Unfortunately, they still had in mind the recent game and guess what? The soldier in question belonged to the sig's unit. Soooo, I now had to cross a veritable minefield of obstacles from Major Des and his officers and NCOs (with famously long memories) to get to the accused. Bloody lovely!

Okay, Phase One. Gritting my teeth, I jumped into my little, short wheelbase Land Rover - minus windscreen - and drove up the hill to the sigs unit perched on top. Hopping out, I crunched across the gravel to the orderly room, where the sergeant greeted me in a scowling fashion. I recognised him as one of the forward pack in the sigs team; great. Ushered into the Admin Officer's Room, I met Captain Bob Jopling - or irreverently named Joe Pling.

Bob greeted me with a smiling face - the first smile in the unit - an excellent officer. I served with him years later when we worked in Canberra as majors.

He knew why I was there and spoke about the incident regretfully as LCpl (we will call him Warren Simkins), in his view, was an outstanding soldier, a national serviceman, called up while attending Sydney University, doing an Arts Degree.

According to Bob, he was an intelligent and highly competent, no-nonsense soldier, and his arrest had come as a complete shock to fellow members of the unit.

'Could any NCOs and Officers of the unit give him a positive character reference?' I asked.

'Absolutely', Bob said, 'I could line up at least ten for you who will vouch for him'.

Thanking Bob, I left to drive over to the MPs compound to interview my client, held there after his charge.

The captain in charge of the MP Unit greeted me warmly and invited me to go into a comfortable interview room where I could talk to LCpl Simkins.

Simkins entered the room escorted by an MP and acknowledged me with the standard 'salute' without a hat. He was a tall, lean, good-looking young man, looking despondent as he sat down in a chair opposite me. I introduced myself to him and informed him that I would be his defending officer.

He said something like, 'what's the use? I'm going to get two years anyway?' Of course, I could not openly agree with his very self-defeating attitude, so I started taking notes.

He told me that the drugs were sent to him by his brother in Australia and admitted that he had used them occasionally at the Sydney University - 'nearly all students use them there,' he said defensively.

'Did you ask your brother to send them?' 'No. he just thought I could use them.'

'Were they for your consumption, or did you share or sell them to other soldiers?'

'Definitely not. I was keeping the drugs to myself so that I wouldn't get sprung.'

'One of the NCOs whom I worked with closely must have smelt my breath and became suspicious. So, he called in the SIB (Military Police Detectives), they quickly found my stash'.

'Are you prepared to swear an oath that you gave the drugs to no one else in the unit?'

'Yes.'

Right - from this, I had two points; his brother had sent the drugs to him, allegedly not on his request, and they became strictly for his consumption alone.

Next, I asked him about the degree he was doing - 'I completed the first year of an Arts Degree with Sydney University when called up. I could have gotten an extension until I completed it in two years, but I elected instead to join the Army as a National Serviceman and complete the last two years of my degree later. So, my degree is scheduled to start again in March next year after I return to Australia.'

By now, I was becoming impressed with Simkins despite my distaste for his fledgling drug habit. Suddenly a light bulb went off in my head – *I wonder*.

'Corporal Simkins, how soon could you re-enrol in your degree course from now, using your excellent communication facilities in the sigs unit?'

'If I got word to my brother today, I probably could get an urgent return in seven to ten days'.

'Do that now - I'll talk to the OC of this MP Unit and contact Capt Jopling to help you - expect a visit from him very shortly.'

'What use will that be, sir? I'll be doing jail time and won't be able to go to Uni anyway?'

Thinking I might be able to pull it off, although it would need a bit of jockeying to get things into position. If I have proof of Simkins enrolment in the university for the coming March, I might be able to influence The Court Martial Board - yeah, likely.

I decided not to get Simkin's hopes up and tell him my plans. My only confidant would be Bob Jopling, who could ensure the completion of the enrolment forms on time. So many pieces needed to fit together in the puzzle, but I saw a slim chance of helping my client.

I outlined my plan to Bob, he quickly saw the idea and was eager to help though he agreed with me - 'that it was a bloody long shot.'

Also, I asked Bob to line up about five people to give him a character reference from senior NCOs and an Officer or two if possible. 'Can do,' said Bob; he proved invaluable support.

In my following interview with LCpl Simkins, I stressed the need to turn up to the Court Martial immaculate in his uniform - haircut, freshly laundered greens, and spit-polished boots no hat allowed as the 'accused'.

The day of the Court Martial soon came around. By stint of every effort, Bob had managed to get the University Course Enrolment Forms completed and returned to the country. To this day, I do not know how he achieved it.

The Court Martial was set up in a special building and designed to intimidate. MPs were at the door, and a lieutenant staff officer had organised all the paperwork.

The Court Martial Panel consisted of a Senior Major, flanked on his left by a Judge Advocate (with honorary Lt Col Rank) who flew in from Australia to sit on Court Martials to advise the President and ensure all procedures were followed correctly.

A judge in the Australian Civilian Courts usually saw the trip to Vietnam to officiate as a type of 'Swan' and a break from their regular work in Australian Courts.

Two more junior majors made up the panel. They sat on the bench, one on each side of the President and Judge Advocate. Crossed flags were set up behind the bench, as the intention was to create an intimidating atmosphere for the accused. All Officers, including myself, wore Sam Browne Belts, as did the Prosecuting Officer. I had spent a long time making sure my dress was at its best.

A fair few people attended as the case had a good bit of interest - these people took their seats, and the Prosecutor and I stood at the left and right of the room, ready to perform.

To open the proceedings, the President called for the escorting MPs to bring the prisoner in, and they did so - Simkins came in looking very smart in his uniform flanked by two MPs who saluted the Court and stepped back from the prisoner.

The Prosecutor began the case, identifying Simkins, then read out the evidence of his charge.

The President then asked Simkins how he pleaded.

'Guilty', he said quietly.

The President then turned to me and asked me if I had anything to say in mitigating circumstances for his guilty plea.

'Yes, sir,' I said as I rose to my feet to address the Court.

'Initially, I would like to make the point that LCpl Simkins did not request the drugs, but they were sent to him unsolicited by his brother.

Secondly, the drugs were for the individual's personal use only and were not offered to, or shared with, any other members of his unit.

I have spoken at length to NCOs and officers of his unit. My findings were that LCpl Simkins stands highly regarded without exception in his unit. Therefore, I have requested that five members of his unit - two officers and three NCOs - attend this Court today to address you. They will give a character reference for LCpl Simkins and their opinion of his work ethics and general demeanour for the time he has been in the country.

With your permission, I would ask Capt Jopling to come forward and address the Court?'

'Permission granted. Ask Capt Jopling to come in,' the President commanded.

Bob Jopling stepped forward, saluted the Court, and spoke earnestly on behalf of LCpl Simkins for about five minutes.

Bob, followed by his sub-unit commander and three NCOs, gave Simkins a glowing reference.

After the last character referee had left the courtroom, the President addressed me again, 'Have you anything further to add Captain Doohan?'

'Yes sir,' I said, rising to my feet - thinking to myself, *'here goes all or nothing.'*

Picking up the Sydney University Enrolment Document from my desk, I approached the bench saying, 'I would like to draw the court's attention to this Sydney University Enrolment Document of LCpl Simkins for his Bachelor of Arts Course; scheduled to commence in March of this year.

The Court has heard of the high esteem LCpl Simkins held and his inability to control the events of his possession of the drugs. Admittedly he should have destroyed them on receipt, and that is the major and only error he has made.

As is the case with all National Servicemen, LCpl Simkins has given up two years of his life for service to his country and has done so willingly and has served it well and fully to the best of his abilities as we have heard from his referees.

Suppose LCpl Simkins endured the long two-year period of detention as appears to be mandatory in cases concerning drug use. In that case, it will mean that LCpl Simkins will have lost four years of his young life and missed his opportunity to complete his degree and better himself significantly.

I am, and I hope the Court is convinced, that the shock of his apprehension will ensure that LCPL Simkins refrains from drug use for the rest of his life.

LCpl Simkins has pleaded guilty. I urge the court to express leniency in the case of this young man. Thank you.'

The President intoned, 'Thank you, Captain Doohan, that will be all for now - unless', turning to the Prosecutor, 'Do you have any comments, Captain Warring?' 'Uh! No Sir.'

'Right, I'd like to ask to clear the court while the panel considers the sentence.'

Chairs squeak as the audience rose and two MPs move forward to escort the accused outside. The rest of us followed to leave the panel to consider the sentence - the verdict already declared guilty.

We waited nervously outside for almost twenty minutes until the orderly called us back. After everyone sat down, the two MPs escorted the accused inside, who stood with head bowed, waiting for the verdict.

The President addressed the accused: 'LCpl Simkins, the Court has accepted your guilty plea and have noted that you had no control over the reception of the substance involved. You have admitted you should have reported it or disposed of it, but you didn't.' My heart sank at this statement. 'However, the court has taken note of your excellent referees and have considered the facts presented by Captain Doohan regarding your University Enrolment. The Court decides that you be sentenced to eight weeks detention starting now and completed in time for you to commence your course.'

There was an audible gasp around the courtroom. 'That's it, march out the prisoner - the court is closed,' and the panel stood up to file out of the courtroom. We all stood as the panel walked out. Then there was a mass exodus.

Outside the courtroom, the crowd were milling around Simkins, slapping him on the back and shaking his hand. Then, finally, Bob Jopling came over to me, 'You did it, Jim!' 'No, Bob, we did it.' Then we shook hands.

Walking over to Simkins, I shook his hand, and he said, 'I can't thank you enough, sir.' 'Thank your squadron supporters Cpl and do me a favour - Ace your BA Course '.

'I will! I will.'

Back to work - thank goodness that is over - only one more Court Martial to make up before I have paid off my penalty of three Court Martials. It was my second one – three, jeesh, 'nobody gets three!'

After finishing dinner at the Officers Mess, I headed into the annex. While wandering around aimlessly, the Judge Advocate addressed me, saying: 'Captain Doohan, Jim, would you care to join me for a brandy?'

Would I ever? 'Let's go out the front, and we'll sit down for a chat.' The JA said, clutching a bottle of Remy Martin and two brandy balloons in his hands.

We walked out to the front of the annex, perched high up on a sandhill with a splendid view overlooking the base and sat down in comfortable cane chairs. 'I just wanted to talk to you about that case today, Jim,' he said as he handed me a brandy balloon.

'Yes, sir,' I said tentatively, thinking the worst.

'Yes, Jim. I've been to a lot of Court Martials up here, and I believe the defence you gave that young soldier today is the best I have seen from an Army Officer.' 'You don't mean that, sir?'

'Yes, and I am convinced that you should study law when you go back to Australia. You have real talent.'

Flustered and embarrassed, I squirmed in my chair.

'You could get your next posting to Canberra and apply to go to the ANU. They have one of the best law faculties in the country. If you complete the first year, you could apply to the Army to do the law full-time. I am sure they would sponsor you. Upon completing your degree, you could transfer a corps to the legal corps, and if you like, I will give you a reference.'

My head spun- 'Thanks, sir. I will talk it over with my wife. It sounds like a terrific opportunity.'

'Drink up and enjoy your brandy.'

I swilled the brandy around and warmed it with my hands, sipping it slowly as I thought, *'Wow! How good would that be?'*

We talked pleasantly for another fifteen minutes before I excused myself and left to walk back to my unit's quiet room with my head whirling. 'Yes! Yes! I could be a lawyer!'

I burst into the quiet room to confront the scene with our old major sitting on a bar stool leaning back with the two front legs off the ground. He had his head buried in a great crown of foam in his pint glass.

'How did the Court Martial go, Jim?' He asked incuriously, glancing over his shoulder; I edged into the room, my swollen head just fitting through the door.

'Great, I got him off with just eight weeks. The JA was so impressed with my defence. He just had a brandy balloon with me and told me I should become a defence lawyer,' I said importantly.

I added pompously, ' I think I'll ask for a posting to Canberra and start studying for a law degree as soon as I get back to Australia. I want to become a lawyer.' I finished triumphantly.

The major's bar stool's front legs crashed to the ground - a great splash of froth blew off the top of his glass, went across the bar and smeared the mirror behind it.

'YOU DON'T WANNA BE ONE OF THOSE BASTARDS, DO YOU?'

I now have a double major maths degree.

THE ROMAN NIGHT

The lead up to The Roman Night is quite extensive as it started two and a half years beforehand.

I worked in Defence Logistics and Planning in Building K, Russell Offices Canberra, which was part of the administrative headquarters of the Australian Defence Force. Quietly working, minding my own business, I received a phone call from my mate Paul Flanagan. He was the postings officer in the Corp's Directorate in Campbell Offices. He asked a legitimate question.

'You're doing a Maths Degree, aren't you, Jim?'

'Yes,' I answered warily.

'Great, well, you are ideal for taking over as SO2 Travelling and Subsistence in the directorate.'

'Paul - I'm doing maths, not bloody accountancy, and no thanks.'

Then the wheedling started, 'Jim, if you take on this job, the Director and I will promise you the job of your choice in two years after you finish your posting.'

Now that was something, 'the job of my choice?' My head spun as I started doing the maths - as you might say. 'I'll take it.'

If ever there was a lemon of a job, this was it - managing a $300m travel budget for the entire Army with little control over the expenditure - just holding the purse strings and carefully monitoring the spend.

For years, the annual cycle had been the same; early in the calendar year, the funds dwindled, the word went out, 'stop, we are running out of money.' Everything screeched to a halt then, and underspend loomed - 'Spend, spend,' a spurt of travel, then, 'stop, stop,' again as the funds became dangerously low. This see-sawing had been going on for years, and it was blatantly apparent that it needed to change.

My staff and I set out to study the problem, and we realised that it was a simple psychological problem. The smaller headquarters and units out in the field had no idea how big or small the money bag was, so they spent blindly with the resultant screeching see-saw.

We reasoned that we needed to give each headquarters a bag of money each year - based on their previous year's expenditure - and let them micromanage it. Then, all we had to do was to keep back a reserve to plug up holes when unexpected over or underspends occurred in junior headquarters - simple solution.

Armed with this new concept, I met with the Director-General Material (a brigadier) to push our theory. He was a switched-on operator and saw right away that we had produced a winner and convened a meeting, calling in all the commanders from the various headquarters to detail the new plan.

The meeting went well, with almost all nodding their heads in agreement as they saw the new system's advantages. But unfortunately, there was one firm holdout, a brigadier from Adelaide, who had a considerable background in the movement sphere. 'Centralisation is the only way,' he intoned, with a rising edge to his voice.

It was then that my good snivelling skills abandoned me, and I 'took him on', knowing that the great brigadier from Mat Branch and my own Lt Col would back me. No such luck, for as I ground away showing the past problems, the brigadier from Adelaide went redder and redder in the face and started to fume. The worst thing was, I was on my own -no one backed me up - they just sat there watching the hard-hitting 'ping pong' match taking place.

The chairperson put the subject to a vote. My system unanimously supported, except for one fuming, significant holdout, the Adelaide Brigadier, who stormed out of the meeting and flew back to Adelaide, where he had three weeks off with high blood pressure.

I shrugged it off at the time, but little did I know that my failed snivel would cost me one year's seniority later. The brigadier sat down and penned a 'black letter'- one that is unseen by the subject officer but goes on your file and trotted out at the Promotion and Selection Committee Meetings when discussing the officer concerned. So illegal and the system stinks, the officer in question has no chance to defend himself. Shown to me from my file years later; in short, the letter said that I should never receive any promotion above the rank of Major, rant – rant, and as he had been Corps Director, my fate was sealed.

Soon after this, I received my posting as I had completed my two-year stint. Ironically, my replacement introduced my proposed system and was awarded an AOM for solving a long-standing problem.

At the end of my stint, rubbing my hands looking at my next salubrious posting - I was tossing up between CTMO Adelaide and CTMO (Chief Transport and Movements Officer) Perth. Perth beckoned, and my wife was eagerly looking forward to it. The outgoing incumbent was my good friend Brian Irving, visiting Canberra. June and I latched onto him and took him out to a restaurant in Manuka, Canberra. We discussed schools and information relative to a transfer in that area and were overly excited from the night.

The following day, Brian marched into the directorate and demanded to know his posting. 'You're not going anywhere,' was the answer. 'You better tell Jim Doohan that. He thinks he's going to take my job.'

A couple of months earlier, I had filled out my Confidential Report answering the questions 'where do you want to serve?' I had written enthusiastically 'Perth or Adelaide'. Where do you not want to serve? 'I don't want to go to Sydney, specifically Holsworthy'.

As I came to work that morning, the postings officer said, 'Jim, I need to speak to you'.

As I sat down in his office, he cleared his throat a couple of times and said, 'You're not going to Perth. Another officer has claimed the posting on compassionate grounds as his wife is a Perth-born woman dying of cancer and wants to go home to her family.' How could I protest that?

Clearing his throat more times, he said, 'Umm, you have been posted as OC 1 Transport Squadron, Holsworthy.'

'WHAT? I was promised a posting of my choice after doing the Travelling and Subsistence job. I put in my last report that I specifically did not want to go to Holsworthy, Sydney! Why can't I have Brisbane where my family is?' 'Col Clues has got that,' he said blandly, 'also the director wants to talk to you about this posting.'

Soon after that, I was ushered into the Director's Office and sat down, still very resentful about the posting. The director began soothingly, 'Jim, we have specially selected you to become OC of 1 Tpt Sqn as you are the most experienced transport squadron officer of your rank in the corps. You have had postings as 21C of a squadron in Newcastle and Operations and Training Officer in 18 Coy RAASC Brisbane, followed by the Operations and Training officer in 5 Coy RAASC in Vietnam. Hence, as a senior major, we figured you are the man we want to go to 1 Sqn RACT in Holsworthy.'

'What's wrong with the squadron?' I asked warily. 'It's, um, not travelling well,' he said lamely. 'I've had a phone call from the Brigadier commanding 1 Task Force. He gave me a rundown of some pretty significant problems, extremely poor EIS (Equipment Inspections), reports of a pistol missing from the armoury, and generally a poor vehicle availability, as well as pretty poor morale among the troops.' Then he added, 'there has been a disproportionate number of charges made against the troops, and overall, the squadron 'needs a senior major to take charge.' My ego was well-stroked at this comment.

'In addition,' he said, 'we have been putting junior majors on promotion in charge of our squadrons. But from now on, our Officers Commanding will be selected from senior majors.'

I left his office, mollified but still dreading the prospect of going to Holsworthy - the backend of the earth, in my view.

Some days later, I received a phone call from a mystery person identifying himself as 'Col cough, cough, er hum!' It obliterated any chance of identification. Later, I would find that he was, in fact, a general.

'Is that Major Doohan?' in a very stern voice. 'Yuh, yes sir,' I stammered. 'Sergeant Willis will not be changing corps from infantry!' he stated firmly. 'Who's Sergeant Willis?' He's a troop sergeant in 1 Transport Squadron and will not be changing corps!'

My good snivelling technique cut in: 'Of course not, sir, I will be incredibly pleased to have an infantry sergeant in one of my troops.' 'Very well, that will be all major.' The last was slightly threatening, and he hung up. My hand was still trembling as I put down the receiver. There was no way in hell I would ask this mysterious Willis to change corps to Transport, and I would fight tooth and nail against any pressure from my corps HQ to stop it.

Weeks later, we moved from our brand sparkling new, four-bedroom home with ensuite, pride and joy in Canberra to Liverpool, a shabby part of Sydney. My wife was eight months pregnant with our fourth child, and unfortunately, there were no four-bedroom quarters available in Hammondville next to the Holsworthy base. Consequently, we spent four weeks in a family room in a motel in Liverpool, waiting for a quarter whilst my wife's time got closer and closer. An absolute nightmare scenario and the worst of the fourteen moves we made in the Army. I also had to take the reins of the squadron, and it was in poor condition indeed.

People on CB, and many of them, could drive into Liverpool at night and go to the hotel. The private cars were parked haphazardly all around the place, and there was no 'Visitors' Car park'. There was a bush fire emergency in the Mittagong area just after I took over. Our Transport Squadron was tasked to link up with the Cavalry Regiment and head to the scene starting at 0700 hrs the following day.

I went to the squadron lines at about 2400 hrs that night and met up with my new 2IC. As it was a captain's job, I briefed him and headed home, expecting him to stay on the job and organise. However, he had different ideas and went back to bed, arriving sleepily at the squadron at 0500 hrs. I had come back down at 0400 hrs expecting the place to be humming, but nothing was ready, and I was testy with him.

The take-off was a disaster. More than half the trucks would not start - I had to jump-start eight of them from my car. The mechanics had to work on the others for hours to get them going. The result was the convoy didn't leave until 1100 hrs vs the 0700 hrs required. Of course, I received a tremendous reprimand for this and could only reply that I had just taken over and it would not happen again.

When the vehicles returned from the bushfires about ten days later, only nine trucks out of forty were available. There are five trucks per section; one of these trucks is fitted with a HIAB Crane to facilitate the unloading of pallets and heavy loads on all trucks in the section. But, unfortunately, none of the HIAB Cranes were working.

The previous OC distinguished the squadron by having all team members participate in the 'Sydney to Surf Run' in full kit. Never mind the vehicles; the obsession was with running fitness. So, all squadron members had to join in the hourly run first thing every morning, and after showering and getting ready, then commence the REAL work.

It meant that the seventeen-man workshop lost 127.5 person-hours per week when they should have been fixing vehicles. I scrapped their requirement for the run over the Ops Officer's vigorous protests. I snarled at him 'look at your bloody availability; your job is to have your trucks fit first'. He saw the logic and agreed.

Next, I was in my office, and I heard the CSM addressing the assembled troops on the parade ground. The hairs stood up on the back of my neck as I heard him berating the troops - straight out bullying. I reached for the phone and rang the directorate in Canberra, 'get this CSM out of here today and send me a good new CSM.'

I never saw that CSM again, and a week later, my new CSM arrived. (The CSM is a vital cog in a squadron, and he and the OC should work hand in glove to run the unit). The CSM they sent to me was the best WO2 I served with in my entire career. He was a small, tidy chap with a quiet voice and presence that the troops respected and admired.

It was not long before he had the unit in the palm of his hand. He had served in AMTDU and was familiar with helicopter landing control and directions. Later, this became obvious when the Divisional Commander and the Task Force Commander landed their helicopter (piloted by the Div Commander) on the squadron parade ground. The CSM skilfully and professionally guided him onto the tight space with the white-faced Task Force Commander in the jockey seat. I still bless the directorate for sending him to me.

One of my first orders instructed that all work stops and privately owned cars parked the same way, facing out. It was because transport trucks had to move forward from their parked position instantly - nose inward did not cut it. So, they may as well practice this while parking their cars each day. It had two desirable effects, it had them thinking about how to park their trucks, and it also made the area look much tidier with all cars facing the same way. So next, I grabbed the RP Corporal and had him organise a proper 'Visitors' Car Park' with appropriate signage.

The previous OC had ordered the RAEME Flag removed from the workshop flagpole and had commandeered the workshop Combi Parts Vehicle for his personal use in place of his issued Land Rover. So, I sent the Combi back to the workshop, told them to put up their flag and demanded to know where the OC's Land Rover was. 'Oh, it's been in the workshop for months now,' said the then driver.

I called the ASM in the workshop: 'I want my Land Rover up here today by 1400 hrs. I don't care what you have to cannibalise to fix it - stop work on all other vehicles until it's fixed!'

At precisely 1400 hrs, a Land Rover appeared canopy flapping wildly, in a filthy condition. 'Got your Land Rover, sir,' the driver exclaimed in a loud voice. 'Is this the way you present the OC his vehicle corporal?' 'Uh, nah, no sir.' 'You're sacked. Get out of the vehicle, and I'll get another driver!' 'What about my trunk?' 'Carry it!' The driver had previously left me unimpressed with his poor dress and attitude anyway - this was an excuse to get rid of him

I got on the phone and requested that the platoon commanders send me their best driver up to my office, and I would promote him and make him my driver.

The new driver arrived- a great soldier and driver. Within three weeks, he had the Land Rover, the best vehicle in the Task Force and nearly drove the workshops mad in the process.

The Offices were long buildings with about four offices per building. My Office was at the end of the building nearest the parade ground, then the next office to mine was the 2IC, then the CSM and RP Corporal on the other end of the building.

It did not suit me as my assistant was the CSM, not the 2IC. So, I swapped the CSM and the 2IC over. However, this still did not suit as the CSM needed a side door through our dividing wall to conduct Orderly Rooms for the many miscreants that manned the squadron. So, we had a doorway built between the CSM's Office directly to mine.

Now I was set up and ready to start functioning correctly. I called my administrative Officer in to see me. 'Right, this will be the procedure; you will draft all replies to correspondence for me and submit them with papers to sign at 1500 hrs each afternoon. The CSM and I will be prowling around most of the day, but I will always be here for you at 1500 hrs, OK?' He was 'fight to get' material. 'Yes, sir.'

Now to tackle the other problems. I started to sift through my in-tray and found dozens of trivial charges awaiting my attention; there was sixty of them. So I called the CSM and asked him to bring the NCOs into my office for a talk.

'Why so many charges? Why can't you give them extra duties or something?' 'Can't do that, sir. It is illegal.' 'Right from now on we will call it 'extra training,' for example: cleaning the toilets will be 'hygiene training,' - use your imagination, and I will support you'.

'Now the other more serious charges. Why are the same people re-offending?' The CB doesn't bother them. They sneak out from the barracks and go to town when they want, ensuring they are here for the specified parades. Punishment doesn't worry them.'

'They are field force soldiers, aren't they?' 'Yes.' From now on, the RP Corporal will erect a tent in front of the Guard

Room; they will sleep there in their field gear while on CB'. I added, 'Furthermore, they will be doing kitchen duties at the Task Force Headquarters during their CB period, which will save our other drivers from doing it.'

Stunned silence, I could see the NCOs drinking this in - the task Force Commander considered me cruel, and the dental unit sent all their miscreants down to my unit to do CB. Following this, charges shrunk from the low twenties per month to one or two. Those forced to camp in front of the Guard House studiously avoided the area and visibly shuddered when walking past it.

Next, I had to tackle the tardiness of our unit in moving out. My subalterns had each received several duty officers for arriving late to work. I didn't accept the British logic of letting the NCOs run the unit while they had a casual breakfast and sauntered down to their units, hours after the soldiers were required to start. The Commandant from Portsea had repeatedly instilled in me the need to lead by example, which included being there at the expected arrival time of the troops. It was not negotiable.

The disastrous convoy on the way to the bushfires around Mittagong left me with a determination to instil in the squadron the major principles of the Transport Corps. They were: Be at the right place, configured correctly for the task and most importantly, AT THE RIGHT TIME!

To emphasise the last principle on the next parade, I announced that the whole squadron had to be mobilised to cross a selected start point at 0700 hrs starting the following Monday morning. If the entire squadron could not make it on time, it would be Tuesday morning at 0630 hrs, then Wednesday at 0600 hrs.

The route the CSM, Ops Officer and I maliciously selected went right past the Task Force Officer's Mess just before a 90-degree turn into the street where the designated Start Point was about a kilometre away. Of course, the 90-degree turn meant that the trucks had to change down right opposite the Officer's Mess with a resultant loud revving and grinding of missed gears from the young drivers a frequent occurrence. The convoy consisted of about forty-eight vehicles and the packets of five, separated by five minutes and interspersed with five or six Land Rovers.

Those figures should have been there if the squadron's vehicle availability was at full strength. But, at that stage, it was only sixty per cent, that is twenty-nine vehicles in convoy.

The Monday morning's effort was abysmal. The first vehicle did not pass the start point until just after 0730, and then the ragged packets drifted past sporadically in an abject showing - Tuesday morning's start was 0630 hrs.

Slight improvement, the first vehicle made the 0630-time, packets scattered and no five-minute timing between the incomplete packets, no way satisfactory. Wednesday morning start time 0600 hrs.

This time was much better, first vehicles right on time, good spacing then, what is this? A packet of two vehicles followed right on the five-minute mark, with a packet of eight vehicles. So, I rang the troop commander, 'Nice try, Mr James, take two Duty Officers'. Thursday morning's start time will be 0530 hrs.

'Good, good, good. - OK, pack it in, Ops Officer. I think they've got the message.'

By now, magically, the squadron started to transform itself. I had sacked six drivers out of the Army; one for incompetence - unable to control his vehicle. The other five for my pet hate - bullying. Discharge from the Army is relatively easy - as there is no point in passing on an incompetent or bullying soldier to another unit to create a problem for them. If the recalcitrant shows no improvement, the Army can do without their services.

The discharge procedure consisted of a first charge punishment and a warning not to re-offend. If the soldier re-offends again in the same manner, an automatic discharge occurs. Usually, these soldiers had been wallowing around at the bottom of the troops leading others astray and thumbing their noses at authority. However, the rapid discharges had the rest of the would-be troublemakers sitting up and taking notice.

The words: Fair, Firm and Friendly were always adhered to, and troops always responded to that.

When one analyses what goes on at the 'quarry face' or where 'the rubber hits the road', very apt in a transport squadron, the Officer Commanding does not know what is happening in their unit. Knowing this, I convened regular 'Corporals only meetings'. These meetings consisted of the CSM and I and all the unit's corporals. I aimed to find out what was going on in the unit and the problems which needed fixing.

The first meeting was a dead failure; the corporals felt intimidated, and only one brave person from the Supplies Platoon spoke up on a troubling aspect. After speaking, I turned to my CSM and said, 'see if you can fix that CSM'. So that was it, meeting closed.

A week or so later, at the next meeting, some more problems arose but were quickly solved by the CSM, or stupid irritating rules changed.

By week three, I could hardly shut them up - now the corporals realised that they were running the unit, not me (in a manner of speaking). The best type of ruler, according to the Chinese Sage Lao Tzu, who says: 'when the job's finished, the workers say, 'we did that,'' and the ruler is an unseen guiding hand.

As a Field Force Squadron, young drivers were on a rotating roster to get field force experience and then posted to other units. Hence, there was a continuous demand for postings into the squadron. Unfortunately also, the posting out of good drivers - against their will. Earlier on, I recall a confrontation by a frantic young driver who pleaded with me to let him stay in the squadron. His main argument was, 'I will never get another sergeant as good as Sergeant Willis again, sir. - Please let me stay!'

Here was that mysterious Sergeant Willis again - I had seen him briefly, and just recently, he had taken acting command of A Troop as the 2Lt OC had been posting out, and we were waiting for his replacement from the RACT Training Centre. So next time I had an O Group, I intended to get Sergeant Willis on his own and have a good talk to him.

The O Group occurred a couple of days later, and I asked Sergeant Willis to stay behind. 'What was the fuss about, I wondered?' The NCO who appeared before me would have to be the worst dressed infantry NCO I had ever seen. He was stocky with short-cropped grizzled hair, a pockmarked tan face and skin, overweight with the buttons straining over his belly and his uniform though clean, hung off him in a shambolic fashion.

I decided to ask him his background; he had recently come from the transport section of 5/7 RAR - he had failed one of their stringent Physical Fitness Tests, and the option of a transfer to 1 Transport Squadron was the only course open to him. Before joining the Army, he had been a rodeo buck jump rider in Queensland near Rockhampton. But, most importantly, he was General Gray's driver as a corporal in Vietnam.

'Aha!' So that is who the caller was? 'Well, I said soothingly, you won't need to change corps while I'm here, sergeant.' My brow sweated as I thought of the good general's reaction otherwise.

We talked for a while, and he was hesitant to speak at first but gradually warmed up. I did not know it then, but I realised later that I had been talking to the best sergeant I was ever to meet in the Army.

As time went on, he, the CSM and I had much to do with each other. Sergeant Willis was the go-to man for every difficult way-out job that came up. His troops thought the world of him. He had a raspy voice, and the minute he called out to any of his drivers, they responded 'on the double'. Of course, their biggest fear was a bawling out by him for waywardness, but he never laid any charges, and his troops would follow him anywhere and, as the saying goes, 'would charge hell with a bucket of water', if he asked them.

A couple of weeks later, I had a phone call from the directorate to tell me that my new troop commanders were arriving. 'Now Jim, we are giving you an excellent Officer, a Portsea Graduate. He was outstanding on his corps' courses, and all his instructors spoke extremely highly of him.' I categorised him as a 'good sniveller' on this report - time would tell.

'Um', the SO1 postings from the directorate went on to say, 'the other officer is just the opposite an RMC graduate who has a chip on both shoulders - he shouldn't have graduated from the training school, bad reports on every course. So, we sent him to you, Jim, to sort him out or, in short - get rid of him -knowing your reputation.' Yeah, nice - what reputation?'

The phone call had barely finished when I reached for the phone again and called up Sergeant Dave Willis. 'Hi, Dave, come up and see me, will you'.

Minutes later, Dave arrived, saluted me, and settled tentatively on a chair in the office corner.

'Dave, we are getting two new officers in the next week or so – one reported to be an excellent young officer and a graduate from Portsea, the other is a Duntroon graduate, and I shouldn't tell you this, but he has a few problems. So, I am sending him to you, Dave!'

'That'd be bloody right, sir!'

Ignoring the comment, I said: 'this is strictly between you and me, Dave, but the minute he acts up or tries to give you a tough time, you come straight to me. Don't worry about any chain of command'.

'OK, Dave. That will be all. I'm leaving it to you.'

'Right, sir,' he said, mumbling to himself as he walked out.

Six weeks after the officer in question marched in, I called Sergeant Willis aside; "How's that young officer going, Dave?' 'He's a bloody bewdy, sir!'

How do you get a sergeant like that?

It, of course, happened following 'The Roman Night', described in the following paragraphs.

Earlier, as the unit's morale started to rise and the officers started to walk around with a bit of a swagger in their step, I received a god-sent opportunity to focus the unit's officers. A flyer arrived from the Task Force Officer's Mess announcing 'A Roman Night' for a forthcoming Saturday.

I cast my mind back to a 'Roman Night' that we had at Portsea, and the costume that impressed the crowd and me most was the Kiwi Red Beetson's outfit - a leper - straight from the movie Ben Hur. It did not take me long to convince the officers of the sheer impact such an outfit would have on the ordinarily staid Roman Nights we had attended in the past.

I contacted our friends from the Dentist Unit (us smaller units had banded together as a counterweight to the Regiments and Battalions in the Task Force). The dental unit officers were enthusiastic supporters of the night and suggested using surgical gloves filled with wet sand as a theatrical extra.

We camouflaged the rear wheels of our six-wheeled drive trucks with hessian daubed with cam paint and wrapped just below the canopy for unrolling when the vehicles were in hiding. These hessian rolls inevitably became caked in dust and had cam paint on them for better effect. So perfect, we would fashion our outfits from them, tie the hessian around the waist with a green toggle rope, put on old worn-out thongs and use cam paint on our faces. What could be better than that?

Now one of the officers with a comprehensive knowledge of Roman History and the treatment of lepers - warned us that we would have to have a separate area at the Mess just for the 'infected lepers'. Also, when walking amongst others, lepers had to chant 'unclean, unclean,' and one of the numbers had to walk in front, ringing a bell so that the gentry could get out of the way.

Furthermore, he pointed out as it was supposed to be a Roman night, we could hardly use the English pronunciation of 'unclean.' A feverish hunt through old Latin schoolbooks showed the Latin word for unclean was 'sordid'. Therefore, as it was the nominative case, we would have to use the word 'sordidus' when referring to ourselves.

So, we went around practising our pronunciation of 'sordidus' in unison until we got it exactly right.

Next, our admin officer rang up the mess secretary and informed him that a party of nine lepers would be attending the Roman Night in the Mess. To protect the other guests, we would need a roped off area proclaimed as 'The Leper Colony' with bold signs all around it warning the other guests of the 'threat' of contamination.

Our partners/wives, horrified at our costumes, refused to travel or be seen with us, going to or coming from the Mess. So, they made their way en masse on the night in a bevy of cars, half-hour before the 'lepers' arrived. Us lepers travelled up to the Mess in a small fleet of Land Rovers about a good half hour later when we expected the party to be in full swing to ensure we maximised our impact.

On arrival, we clambered out of the Land Rovers and assembled in loose formation with the bell ringer in front.

We each carried a sign and had to call out 'sordidus' on approaching people without leprosy.

As we approached the Mess entrance, the Mess Secretary, with a wry smile, opened the door to let us shuffle in, loudly calling out 'sordidus' and waving our signs above our heads. The bell ringer was clanging vigorously in front of us. The Mess Secretary, God Bless Him, had said nothing to the other guests about the 'lepers' - though I suppose other guests gazed at the roped off area with 'leper' signs all around it and wondered.

When we shuffled into the Mess shouting, the guests seated in various Roman types of arrays on cushions on the floors gazed open-mouthed at the spectacle. One lady in a red backless dress had her back to the entry corridor as we entered—a dentist officer - who shall remain nameless. - could not resist such a tempting target and, as he passed said lady, dropped one of his cold wet sand-filled glove 'hands' down her back with a slurred mutter of 'pardon my hand lady'.

The victim gave a tiny gasp as she felt the cold, wet lump slide down her back and, reaching around, grabbed it, and looked at it. Then, when she saw what it was, she let out a shriek and flung it across the room where it landed in the lap of her friend opposite - another shriek, and things were getting decidedly agitated for a while.

The column wended its way into the roped-off area and settled down on some old bags spread on the floor for us - the mess secretary said that lepers could not expect cushions - our wives were in an area on cushions close by and glared at us.

Of course, there was no wine for us lepers, just jugs of beer that we quaffed in quantity. Nevertheless, our entry had livened up the show, and as the night progressed, other attendees started to drift into the leper enclosure to join us. So that is where the action was.

By the end of the night, most guests were in the leper colony area, and all had a rousing time.

The Wash-up:

One woman had a bad asthma attack - the first one she had had since a child - blamed it on the hessian. We all lepers developed a rash from the hessian that lasted for days.

But one thing was sure, 1 Transport Sqn had arrived and made our presence felt in the Task Force. All the squadron officers now walked with a jaunty step and were laughingly proud of their escapade.

CPSIA information can be obtained
at www.ICGtesting.com
Printed in the USA
LVHW010324070422
715519LV00008B/146

9 780645 404210